SPIRITUAL SURFING

Riding Life's Turbulent Waves to Victory

JAMES L. CATANZARO, PH. D.

Spiritual Surfing: Riding Life's Turbulent Waves to Victory

ISBN: Softcover 978-1-936912-80-3

Copyright © 2013 by James L. Catanzaro

To order additional copies of this book, contact:

Southern Collegiate Press

1-423-475-7308

www.parsonsporchbooks.com

Southern Collegiate Press is an imprint of Parson's Porch & Company (PP&C) in Cleveland, Tennessee. PP&C is an innovative non-profit organization which raises money by publishing books of noted authors, representing all genres. All donations from contributors and profits from publishing are shared with the poor.

Contents

FOREWORD

DOWN THROUGH THE CENTURIES, PEOPLE of the world have yearned for a more peaceful and harmonious world. On January 1, 2000, an editorial in The New York Times captured the hopes and imaginations of Americans in a new millennium:

> ". . . in these first few hours of a new era, it behooves us to imagine the future with a sense of optimism, something that eluded our ancestors as they struggled just to survive. We have the humane vision and the technological means to lift the world family to new levels of liberty, affluence, health and happiness. Forging that possibility into reality is the task that greets us in the morning of the new millennium."

Dr. James Catanzaro has taken up the challenge. He has gone in search of a way to lift us all to a life "above the struggles." He had a hunch that there is an undiscovered power within individuals that can be tapped for the good of humanity. In his search, he has talked to literally hundreds of interested people—a purposive sample, not a random sample, including people of evident virtue all across the United States, who are searching for the better life: the life above the struggles.

Dr. Catanzaro "listened with his heart" as well as his mind and after hours of reflection, bit by bit, his thoughts settled into a configuration that gave him the insight of a metaphor that carries the theme of the book: surfing!

In essence, this book explains, step by step, how one can be carried forward as on a great wave, experiencing a positive feeling that lifts one "above life's struggles." This experience Dr. Catanzaro calls *Scend*. (See his definition on page 20.) It grants perspective on life, an inspired attitude that turns the struggles into strength-building challenges, and raises human beings to a higher level of living.

Is the surfing metaphor real? According to the sample of people Dr. Catanzaro interviewed, there is a phenomenon of "being carried forward as if by a great wave." Seventy-nine percent of Dr. Catanzaro's sample said they knew someone who had been carried forward as if by a great wave. Thirty-four percent said they had personally experienced being carried forward as if by a great wave.

Scientists are schooled to be skeptical, but, when a phenomenon occurs, the question is not whether to deny or to believe but rather how to investigate, discover, and explain. The evidence is that Dr. Catanzaro has discovered the phenomenon *Scend*. He explains to us, step by step, how to achieve *Scend* and, thereby, how to achieve spiritual well-being.

This book is a manual for spiritual surfing, for being Scent from struggle to spiritual well-being. It can lift the world family to new levels, to . . . ASCEND!

Dr. Donald 0. Clifton, Former CEO, The Gallup Organization

INTRODUCTION

YOU SHOULD NOT HAVE PICKED up this book if a search for happiness and well-being is not underway in your life. Why? Because that's what this book is about.

In the simplest of terms, here's how we will proceed. We'll begin by identifying and scrutinizing our foes which I call "the struggles." And we'll end with robust strategies for victory over these foes, establishing a life powered by spiritual well-being.

Sounds easy, but life struggles aren't easy issues to plumb and resolve; and gaining and sustaining spiritual well-being have eluded most who have searched for it. As for "the struggles," they've been plaguing folks, even people of faith, for at least a century. So, whether you were brought up getting your highs as a child from Bugs Bunny or SpongeBob SquarePants, you know something of these struggles; and, most likely, you know how perplexing and daunting they can be. Actually, the chances are very good that you're still seeking answers to them.

You should appreciate, then, that it's going to take some serious reflection to understand how to get the best of the struggles that befall us, and some serious changes in living to ensure a life of peace and happiness. For me, this has been a life-defining quest. It's a quest much like my passion —finding the waves in a turbulent sea that can take you to the serenity of foam and sand while escaping those that likely will deliver you to panic and pain.

Let me introduce you to this quest. Most of us, at some point, are knocked around by life's tumultuous waves. We struggle. My research shows that it's a nearly universal phenomenon.

We live in a different world from those in past generations. It's a world of amazing speed and extraordinary accommodations to our needs and interests. Nevertheless, only rarely is life "picture perfect" for us, even for affluent Europeans and the multitude of successful peoples in the New World.

Usually life tests us. Most of us have understood this from childhood. Whoever we are, wherever we are, we know there are times when happiness and well-being simply aren't our companions. We run into walls. Our chances for the "good life" — attaining it and keeping it going — are all too commonly compromised.

These trials come on top of the sometimes nasty, nearly universal corrosive effects of living in the 21st century—things like the daily barrage of spam, robocalls, emails and text messages, "friends" saving them and sending intimate ones viral; the ups and definitely the downs of the market; being laid off or under-valued at work; the threat of having our ID's stolen; facing here and there mindless acts of violence and determined acts of terror; a cacophony of political and religious voices; poisonous family disputes; aggravating traffic jams; colds and the flu when you least need them; lots of drama. They all can come our way; and they all can wear us down and send us to struggle.

Some stoically endure these assaults; others become anxious, frazzled, ultimately spent. So, with complete justification, many folks these days find themselves overrun by the vicissitudes of life. And if we aren't, we've at least experienced everything from gut-wrenching disappointments to contagions of fear and insecurity. Just think back to 9/11 time! U.S. airports were closed. The President, we were told, was flying from place to place to ensure his survivability. And most every day we heard about threats of terror — even in our own home towns.

All of these experiences tore at our confidence. For many, they punctured their sense of well-being and sent them to struggle.

So whatever our situation, we pretty much know from our own experiences, more often from those about us, surely from those who make the daily news, that struggles can get the best of us. And we grasp that when they do, they block us from the positive outlook and personal fortitude we need to propel ourselves forward in a fast-moving, helter-skelter world. In fact, struggles great and small can alter our entire life patterns, sometimes so dramatically we appear to others as different people. This is abundantly true when catastrophic events overtake us: the death of a treasured child, partner or parent; acute health problems; separation from a lover or divorce; the loss of a job, a career, our financial base. The list of life-crushing calamities we know to be virtually endless.

Yes, but despite all this grit in our lives, despite the threat of monumental setbacks, for some, even moments of total desperation, despite all these struggles, we also know that . . .life can be an ongoing rush. It can be like going to the beach on an early summer day . . . beautiful!

How our struggles can be mapped and then overcome to bring us to sunny happiness will be detailed in the pages that follow. To reveal how the struggles and strategies are worked out in daily living, we'll be very direct, not mincing any words. We'll paint the picture honestly, sometimes starkly — because this is what it will take to get us free of the struggles.

We'll also use story-telling here and there to flesh out our principal points. It's a powerful form of conveying the serious and the profound. Sometimes we only get the message when we hear it played out in life situations. So I've mixed in with researched observations reminiscences from a number of my life journeys. It's the approach early Christian writers took as they framed the gospel, as they sought to elevate the spiritual standing of those following Christ. It clearly is the way ancient Jewish writers told of their God and their role in his world.

So, in this book, our search for spirituality will take us from being overwhelmed at times by the waves of life to riding them to safety and gaining our fair share of happiness.

How am I qualified to scope out such large issues and offer truly effective answers? I came at formulating strategies for overcoming struggle and granting spiritual well-being through a myriad of powerful experiences. My doctoral studies in philosophy of religion began the process. Then, over decades, I had a series of focused conversations with a host of noted scholars and clerics who delivered some compelling insights. But what put all these lessons about life together into an action plan was the research done with a special friend, Dr. Don Clifton, who was then the recently retired CEO of The Gallup Organization, an internationally celebrated research psychologist, and the leader of the Positive Psychology movement.

Together we surveyed nearly 500 Americans selected to mirror anticipated readers (those in search of spiritual well-being). As it turned out, a few in our sample said they were already models of spiritual strength. Struggles were no longer bringing them down. We separated these folks out and scrutinized their responses to determine common traits and commitments.

Then came the key phase of our research project: many respondents were engaged in focus groups along with hundreds of others to explore in depth what people believed had sent them into struggle and, for some, what they felt enabled them to break free and live above struggle.

From reflecting on this intensive and extensive body of work we became confident of this:

Wherever we are in life, whoever we are, there are strategies we can use that will lead us forward using the power of life's natural waves to carry us past struggle to emotional and spiritual well-being.

It's a transformed life we seek, one that taps continuously into the reservoir of strength within us. It's a life where peak experiences define our common experience, and openness, trust and forgiveness are ever-expanding.

"Don't struggle over anything," wrote the Apostle Paul, "but in all things—through prayer and supplication coupled with thanksgiving—make your requests known to God.

And the peace of God that is beyond all understanding will guard your hearts and minds through Christ Jesus" (Phil. 4:6-7).

CHAPTER 1
THE SURFER'S CHALLENGE

IT WAS A BRIGHT SPRING DAY AND, lucky me, an avid surfer, I was on Manly Beach just outside Sydney, Australia. When you arrive by ferry you are greeted by a hundred-foot long marble wall with these words carved on it: "Manly Beach . . . Seven miles from Sydney, a thousand miles from care." That tells it all! Manly is a great place to leave your cares behind — at least most of the time.

The surf was up the day I arrived, but, as I was informed at the espresso shop, it was a humongous red flag day. The sea was off-limits! Well, it was my only day on Manly, so I ignored the admonitions and headed directly to the beach to take on the giant waves everyone was fretting about.

Now, as a practice, I don't put my wetsuit on the right way. I like the zipper on the front, not the back. I like control of what's attached to me! This didn't go unnoticed by the Aussie life guard who cautioned me first about the danger I was facing, and then pointed out that, as a Yankee, I apparently didn't realize what is wetsuit proper as well as the meaning of red flags on a beach. I nodded my thanks for his cautions and pressed on to body-surf the waves. (O.K., I admitted to myself, he was probably right; a board wouldn't have stayed under me long in such treacherous waters and that could spell days of needless pain and frustration.)

While the teenage board riders hung back behind the breakers to escape bone-crushing mountains of water or sat on the beach waiting for better times, I took wave after wave to foam and sand. It was as glorious a day as I've ever spent at the beach! And, to top it off, when I finally came out of the water —totally exhausted but entirely euphoric —my life guard friend smiled broadly and yelled to me: "Well, mate, you put on a clinic out there!"

When we successfully take on big challenges in life, we feel on top of the world. We're positive about ourselves and life itself. We see ourselves as victorious; and sometimes others do as well.

Your experience may be different, but whatever it is, you know that life isn't always pacific; it's more like the Pacific! On many days "surf's up" and on some of those days red flags are out and angry waters buffet those who venture into the fray. As a result, as we're walking the beach of life, we may on one day ride the swells to euphoria and on another get caught up in a virtual tsunami. In other words, we can be thrown into struggle — even when we least expect it.

Many are defeated by these bouts with life's struggles. The swirling surf gets the best of them. It pushes them around and pulls them down. They're overwhelmed. Struggle, in fact, ends up defining their lives. They're slugging it out — virtually every day of their lives.

When I began to research this phenomenon, I asked

those who told me they had been overrun by struggles why they thought this had happened to them. Most often they started by relating stories about being worn down by everyday trials, and then went on to talk about nasty events in their lives, and, quite often in strong language, about ugly people who had broken into their lives. Almost always, when pressed further to account for these downturns, they revealed deeper issues — base insecurities, feelings of eroded self-worth, even anger that they had ended up with so few good-life cards dealt to them.

They would say dire things like, "I guess I've lost my way." Or worse, "I just don't know if I'm worth anything to anyone anymore."

Of course, we all tussle with meaning and purpose at some level. To be human is to be aware of our mortality. Most of us recognize that we're living among more than seven billion people on planet earth. We're like a tiny grain of sand on a mile-long beach, a grain that may soon be washed out to sea.

But we also know what often happens when such pessimistic reflections overtake us. We run and hide. Some become consumed with life's tasks, their work, perpetually distracted from their true situation. And some others become consumed by an ideology or a cause. Like cultists, they translate their life events into a divine script and write them off fatalistically as God's will or the devil's doings.

What's the outcome? At some point calamity arrives.

They find themselves with shaken confidence, their sense of well-being punctured, their ability to handle the inevitable downturns in life gutted. Naked and alone they stand.

No doubt they didn't set out on life's journey with this in mind. What they desired all along was something quite different — days flooded with happiness, not struggle; rewarding relationships, not poisonous or trying ones; fulfilling careers, not the grind; and peace mixed with pregnant moments of laughter and large measures of delight and joy.

Whether we're just knocked around a little by life's waves or shaken to the core by the big ones, what do we ultimately desire? At a minimum, to avoid being overrun by the daily stresses and tensions of life, certainly by the setbacks and losses fate sometimes dishes up. Beyond that, we seek a bounty of enriching relationships and rewarding experiences — the good life.

This is what I heard loud and clear from those I questioned in focus groups and surveyed nationwide. They were emphatic. They wanted life's struggles to be reduced to manageable challenges. They wanted to feel aligned with their inner selves, with their partners in life, with life itself. They wanted to live above the fray. They sought an end to struggle.

Many said they desire even more. They long to be aligned with what is greater. They seek spiritual well-being.

I'm one of them. I came to this juncture some time ago. In fact, I've engaged in a spiritual search for much of my adult years — with bumps and bruises along the way. It's been a challenging journey. Many times I felt alone in this search.

The good news is: more and more people are seeking this pathway. In fact, our century, when it's finally recounted, may turn out to be more about our exploration of "inner" space than our pursuit of outer space. Both pursuits, of course, hold promise for humankind, but I am confident of this: mapping our inner space holds the greater promise — for us as individuals, for our loved ones, even for our world.

Of course, lofty aspirations like these are not attained overnight. They don't arrive by Googling them up. Living above struggles, certainly the dark, threatening mountains we sometimes confront, takes thoughtful preparation, some courage, a lot of hard work, and a little luck. Hopefully, we all recognize this and are ready to make the commitments necessary to the task.

CHAPTER II
LIFE'S TURBULENT WAVES

M ARCH DAYS IN COLORADO ARE COOL, but often sunny and clear. If you're in Ridgway near the famous ski resort town of Telluride, they're likely to be enchanted by views of towering, snow-capped mountains. And if you're sitting on the deck of Earthship when day breaks, as I was some years ago, a wondrous quiet can be yours as well. Earthship, you may have heard, was Actor Dennis Weaver's eco-house built into the side of a precipitous hill, fashioned from used tires, empty Coke cans, and mortar.

I was there for several days with this former star of Westerns, now deceased, along with his wonderful wife Gerry and several other guests. On our first morning we became engaged in serious conversation about the prospect of hydrogen-powered cars. This was Dennis' passion at the time. But after an hour or so of intense and, honestly, tiring discussion, I felt I had to rescue Dennis — o.k., myself, as well. So I gently but rudely interrupted with this suggestion: "Let's all go ride horses!" "No, no, Jim," Dennis quickly responded, "I've got business to be transacted first." "Well, Dennis, if it's o.k. with you, I'll go saddle up a horse and explore your property." "That's all right with me," he said, "but we have no horses in the barn." No horses?! "I don't much like riding," he whispered.

You can imagine my amazement. Isn't this the man who starred, limp and all, in two long-running TV Westerns, "Gunsmoke" and "McCloud"? Don't I see pictures around his house of Dennis on location, in parades, out in the countryside — on horseback? "I've been fortunate to have a career on horseback," he revealed, "but also unfortunate." "I've been typecast! I'd rather not ride; I don't much like horses; I'd rather act in Shakespearean plays."

What a revelation!

It's easy, I later reflected, to be typecast — and apparently when that's so, we lose a measure of our authenticity. We have to live out a persona which may very well not be a true reflection of who we are. And, when this happens, our well-being is threatened, even spiritual well-being.

That's heavy stuff because when we speak of spirituality we are referring to the very center of our being.

Now, admittedly, "spirituality" is a relatively new term in Western discourse; so it has a measure of ambiguity attached to it. It has been the centerpiece for New Age writers and followers; and it's made its way into the everyday language of millions of others without much specificity. Its origins may be more Eastern than Western; nevertheless, it describes a state many of all persuasions and heritages say they want to achieve.

I've had the opportunity to interview over fifty leading clerics and scholars who represent the world's major religious traditions. Most all speak about spirituality; however, when I reviewed the recorded interviews, I could see that most all are also not entirely clear what the word conveys.

After years of reflection on this term and gleaning from these authorities what they appear to agree upon, I've settled on this base definition:

"Spirituality is a state of transparent well-being that comes from transforming relationships — with the sacred, with others, and with one's self."

How do these relationships come about? I once was sure they came from right belief, right conduct, and right worship. I was raised to believe this, and virtually all of my early experiences reinforced it.

My parents sent me several summers when I was very young to a wonderful camp in the Muskoka Lakes region of Ontario, Canada. Every evening around a bonfire on the "beach" we heard stories and sang songs which drove home this message. Every morning after breakfast we had Bible study. Right belief, right conduct, and right worship framed the message. It was a wonderful experience with great fellow campers and truly caring mentors and guides, so these messages had force. They also reinforced what I had heard daily at home and every Sunday at church.

I became certain that believing fundamental doctrines of the Christian faith, living a righteous life and going to the right church guaranteed spiritual well-being, the kind that can take you past the nasty struggles of life.

Early in my search for spiritual well-being, I had two life-transforming epiphanies that, when melded together, forever changed that view. The dean of my college— a man with a large adopted family yet modest income, exceptional intellectual attainment, and transparent spiritual depth, an orthodox Christian by anyone's definition—-took me as his "mentee" one arctic winter night to a downtown evangelical church in Boston where he was to preach.

It was an extraordinary experience. After an inspiring service, he surprised everyone present, certainly me, when he bolted past faithful greeters to the rear of the sanctuary and then turned as if possessed to make his way to a vagrant huddled in the corner. Without a moment's hesitation, the dean took his new overcoat and draped it around this hapless man. I was amazed— and warmed! I knew what only a few did: he had saved for this coat for over a year.

It was, for me, powerful, life-defining—a special revelation—not just because of the impact of this monumental sacrificial act of kindness or of the exceptional goodness of this man. It was an experience of feeling the presence of a great, ennobling, inspiring force that had moved him —from his innermost self —to remarkable empathy, care, and generosity. It moved me to reflect on my own spiritual capacity, as well. Compressed into thirty seconds was, I felt certain, the essence of spiritual well-being.

Several years later, I was in for a shock. I found myself the student of a renowned thinker who in so many ways works outside the fold of orthodox Christianity. I was astonished that he, too, exhibited the same compelling, primal force, in virtually every encounter I had with him. As I interacted with him over several years he became for me a model of spirituality.

Reflecting on these powerful experiences turned out to be more transforming than years of study. They brought me to see that when the human spirit is elevated through graced relationships, it transforms lives—ours, and those about us. The human spirit is, indeed, the lamp of God (Proverbs 20:27).

What is so special about this insight? Whatever our faith tradition or our spiritual standing, we are schooled to believe spirituality comes from confessing our weaknesses, then looking to outside authorities for help, rather than celebrating our strengths and releasing the positive power within.

My research into spirituality reveals that most people have witnessed, at least once, inspiring power in others. But here's the kicker: Only a few say they experience that power within themselves. Unfortunately, I've also discovered that most people believe that this power cannot be fully theirs.

Now fast forward to a few years later when I had two further life-defining epiphanies. Exhausted from an all-night flight to England but wishing to be friendly, I offered a meager greeting to the woman behind the hotel check-in counter: "How are you doing?" "Struggling through," she replied. Quite surprised, I countered: "Why would you answer that way?" "That's what we Londoners often say when asked that question." "Tell me why," I continued. "Well, that's what life is, isn't it, a struggle, at least here."

Perhaps, it is, I thought; and after a few days in London, I began to see her point. Of course, American life, especially in our big cities, is no less helter-skelter. We, too, struggle, at times, down to our last emotion— though we typically respond in a more affirmative manner: "Fine," "Good enough," "OK".

A few months after my London trip, I visited New York City. This time it was the woman behind the hotel check-in counter who greeted me with "How are you today?" "Struggling through," I said attempting to gain a revealing response. I did. "You'll find a number of churches nearby; we're known for our churches," she insisted. Obviously, she assumed I had spiritual problems, probably because our struggles in America, like those of the British, so often resolve down to our ongoing search for life's purpose, for what connects us to our innermost selves, to the transcendent— ultimately to what or who will enable us to overcome life's struggles.

More than 75 percent of those I surveyed reported that they were not satisfied with their spiritual lives—that they struggle. That's a very large slice of the adult population!

Other critical findings were uncovered as well: that spiritual well-being and struggle are, in many ways, polar opposites: Overcome "The Struggles" and you will take a significant first step toward spiritual well-being. And this: Build essential connections and you will achieve and sustain spiritual well-being. It's not enough, in other words, to stop struggling. Spiritual well-being materializes when we actively engage in connecting.

CHAPTER III
SIZING UP THE WAVES

S O NOW THAT YOU HAVE THE basic formula of this book, let's go back to the starting place for a moment and make a run at establishing the full significance of the terms thrown about thus far.

Let's start with the most basic term, struggle. What is it actually? It's pushing forward but feeling held back by powerful forces not easily overcome. If they were, we wouldn't have so many folks telling us they're struggling! The fact is, whether we say we are very happy, pretty happy, mildly happy or unhappy, most of us admit in moments of candid honesty — we struggle—especially to gain and sustain well-being.

During the past twenty-five years, research psychologists have uncovered that most Americans— also many people worldwide –report to interviewers that they are happy. Yet most all betray, in the very same surveys, that their daily lives are plagued by troubling setbacks — with intimate partners, in their careers, and, most profoundly, in their search for spiritual well-being. In fact, just as many who claim to be happy reported this as did those who see themselves as basically unhappy!

What can we take away from this conundrum? Clearly this: happy times don't steel us against life struggles. They simply aren't an elixir for overcoming struggle.

Put another way: We just can't smile away deeply rooted feelings of insecurity, isolation, emptiness or gritty day-to-day entanglements.

So, whether we accept the observations of hotel clerks or the findings of social psychologists, whether we're English or American, our everyday experience is usually not idyllic, healing, and transforming. No, more times than not, our daily routine is "struggling through"—slugging it out!

This should not come as a big surprise. Life for most of us is very many times punctuated by experiences we dread. Every day the media and those at the "watering holes" at work or in the marketplace tell of random acts of violence, inexplicable want and devastating loss, conspiracies against us, and unconstrained deception — to say nothing of such mega-threats as nuclear attack, terrorism, pandemics and economic chaos.

Whatever our situation, whatever our history, many fear that change will likely be for the worse; and most of us know that it can come at us like a tsunami — unanticipated, overwhelming, and debilitating. Rather than evolutionary, predictable, and thus digestible, what we believe may befall us is likely to be so abrupt it will come as a punch in the gut.

Real life accounts, accounts we've heard since childhood, make the case in our minds. They tell us, virtually in unison, that disruptive change comes in the night, and most often it's "in your face." Just a moment's reflection on the recent history of the stock market, on the impact of new technologies on our lives, on those who fleece others through the practice of deception, or on the spate of world crises and unpredicted global failures makes this point clear. The big disasters often come with surprise — and so do many of the small ones!

As far as everyday relationships are concerned, we understand they too can easily descend into tumult. The social media inform us daily that relationships frequently need to be re-negotiated and, even then, they can blow up in our faces.

So, as we mature, most of us come to realize there are no magic pills or quick fixes when we run into these troubles—despite therapists of all sorts, exotic spas, purple pill mood elevators, shopping, gambling, alcohol, spiritual gurus of all stripes, and an avalanche of self-help books, blogs and tweets. All of these may deliver brief happiness spikes but virtually all of them drop us back into the doldrums.

And what about our religious lives? Here, as well, we commonly experience the same roller-coaster ride. This is particularly so in traditions which center on person-to-person relationships with God. When God's presence is real, the believer exults; when that presence fades, the believer despairs.

Why this manic-depressive swing? Religion commonly gets us to look to outside sources to save us, to raise our spirits, to carry us through. But here's the dilemma: looking outside doesn't appear to take us to ongoing security, to the spiritual well-being we seek. The outside source of rescue comes and goes. In time virtually all outside grips give way, and nearly always those outside "authorities" – from Pope to pastor to televangelist — disappoint us.

Instead, as we will learn, getting a hold on struggle and attaining spirituality come from making an inside connection — marrying our aspirations to inspiration. This is actually the view of many theologians as well as psychotherapists I've interviewed, and of average citizens we surveyed, though most all are unclear how this might occur.

Then there's the term spirituality. What truly is it? I take it to speak of devotional, sacramental living, care for others, and resilience derived from inner strength in the face of destructive struggle. The major religions of the world are all centered on spirituality — through the devotional community life of Eastern Orthodox Christianity; through the sacramental life of Roman Catholicism; through godly individual living in Evangelical Protestant Christianity; through socially concerned living in Liberal Protestantism; through authentic living for New Age followers; through awakened living in Buddhism; through tolerant living from duty in Hinduism; through submissive living in Islam; and through sanctified living in Judaism.

We speak of spirituality in a host of ways through these religious traditions of the world. But these traditions labor to tell us how to attain and sustain it. This is understandable. Religion derives from personal history, family, ethnicity, culture, station in life. Spirituality, on the other hand, transcends religious traditions and speaks of our experience of what is of "ultimate concern." Nine out of ten of our survey respondents agreed that they have a spiritual dimension, but less than a quarter, spread evenly among those of varying religious traditions, believe they themselves approach spiritual satisfaction in life. They struggle.

CHAPTER IV
FINDING THE SWEET SPOT

NEARLY TWENTY-FIVE HUNDRED YEARS ago, the philosopher Aristotle ventured that the highest of all goods is happiness. But he was quick to offer that we all differ about what happiness is. Ever since, great minds around the world have labored to prove him wrong. They've tried to describe the ultimate happiness . . . but without much success.

In fact, the very nature of human happiness is still debated. I'm convinced that human happiness and spiritual well-being go hand in hand. This merging of spiritual well-being into a description of happiness is new to the West. For the better part of two millennia, our pursuit of the good life in western civilization could be readily traced to the ancient Greeks, while a quite different interest, the pursuit of righteousness, had its origins in the Judeo-Christian ethic.

It's my contention that the two traditions must be brought together if either is to be sustained because happiness and righteousness are essentially connected.

One way to picture the happiness coming from spiritual well-being is to imagine a person who is making evident progress, building on strengths and establishing vital connections. What's powering this progress? A closer look reveals that her forward movement is by inner propulsion. No one or thing is pushing or pulling her. She is energized; she is turning conflict into stimulating give-and-take, setbacks into cushioned falls, and struggle into invigorating challenge. Her countenance is warm and expressive. She is taking charge of her life rather than being taken on by life's ups and downs. Her life has an upward trend line. Contrary to John Cougar Mellencamp, life goes on and the thrill of living stays on.

Of course, our model of spirituality has not reached nirvana. We all run into resistance, stumble, and feel tedium in life. We all encounter forces arrayed against us—our genetic makeup, unlucky timing, aging, actions of people about us . . . And we all recognize that whatever our background, gender, status in life, or most recent birthday, struggles can corner us and take the joy out of life, and they can take the life out of moments of joy.

The good news is that struggles need not shatter our hopes and carry us to "the blues." In a century still filled with hope, yet pregnant with uncertainty, sometimes even mortal threat, we need not answer "How are you doing?" with "struggling through." We can live without being held captive by fear and struggle; we can see the glass as more than half full; we can be empowered; we can be resilient and resourceful.

In fact, perhaps for the first time in human history — given extended life, burgeoning wealth, work without great ardor and pain, time to "smell the roses," instant communication worldwide to alert us to danger and tell us of opportunity — despite all the threats, we can be optimistic; and we can achieve a heightened quality of life, even happiness, indeed, even spiritual well-being.

It's noteworthy that "optimism" as a word was not included in Samuel Johnson's 1755 dictionary. It apparently wasn't a word in use! Much later, in the 19th century, Helen Keller wrote a famous essay on optimism as a young adult but then later conceded that she had lacked insight into human nature when she earlier spoke optimistically about the possibilities of humanity.

Being spiritually whole means speaking and acting from optimism, when we're old as well as when we're young. It's being excited about who we are, where we are right now, and, mainly, where we are going—even if we are not the heroic characters of our adolescent dreams, leading or saving the world.

Being spiritually whole means feeling inspired and being inspired — carried forward as if by a mighty wave. Our research shows this insight to be quintessential to understanding spirituality. It's what is captured by the word "Scend."

What is Scend? In its Old English origins, it's a nautical term that refers to the driving force of the sea, of the spurt forward of a vessel being carried along by a great ocean swell.

As a lifelong body surfer, I understand the Scend of the sea. I know the liberating whoosh, the true exhilaration of being propelled beachward by a powerful wave—to the serenity of foam and sand. It's psychologically — every bit as physically—renewing. It is Scend! And I know how difficult it is to get into position to capture a wave, how every wave in the sea brings new challenge. But I am confident, as well, that each new wave–wondrously—offers new possibilities.

I've experienced Scend also in human relationships. It's bonding with another, soul to soul. It's the "chemistry" that brings life to sublime relationships. I recall the end of a euphoric day of surfing great waves and enjoying with my wife Rhonda the comfort of being alone on the magnificent Crane Beach of Barbados. We picked up our belongings and began our trek to our car nearly a quarter-mile away. Suddenly, from out of the jungle-like brush that borders the beach, a young Bajan man came running. Wonderfully, realizing his appearance could be interpreted by us as threatening, he slowed down, threw up his hands, and shouted, "Don't worry, I'm not an American."

We welcomed his arrival. His exclamation, however, sent us to ponder for weeks to come about what kind of a culture and image we Americans have created. But our unexpected embrace of words and arms that day with our stranger-friend brought to both of us a sense of the human spirit we share. We were carried forward by a warm and healing impulse—Scend—connecting us city folk with a man of the islands.

Spiritual Scend is the power of the sacred expressed in our lives as a surge of positivity and optimism. It's redemptive; it's transforming; it's like a giant healing wave. Being empowered by Scend is being inspired to reach out and embrace others, and, most important, to feel we can overcome most any obstacle through our inner strength.

The Scend experience often comes in a flash, unexpectedly and at momentous times—when people experience triumph, when they connect "soul to soul" with others—for many Christians, when they encounter the caring Jesus as the Christ.

Sometimes, Scend is experienced in the calm of gardening or walking in the rain. Sometimes Scend comes when we're alone with our thoughts or lost in music. Sometimes we feel we're a child of the universe.

Whatever the source, Scend encounters take us to our roots, to deeply embedded values and aspirations, to inner warmth and resolution. Most important, they unite us with others in a common bond, and they color our lives "happy."

Can Scend be our everyday partner? Usually, feeling good about the world is short-lived. Researchers tell us that virtually all big lottery jackpot winners stay euphoric for just a short time. Their new financial standing replaces the old, but, as before, it's insufficient. Expectations have risen even beyond their new means. And soon there are complications: family and friends—close and remote—want a share in their new wealth; many more possibilities pull at the winners; and, in a short time, they aren't clear whether people are with them because they like them or because they want to exploit them. Material pleasure, in any case, proves transitory.

I was sitting on the curb outside a convenience store, enjoying a double-dip ice-cream cone with my four year old grandson, Trey. "What makes you happy?" I asked him. "Eating chocolate ice cream," he replied quickly. A few minutes later came an unexpected request: "Can I throw my cone in the trash?" He still had a scoop to go, but I nodded approval. I recall commenting: "I thought you said eating chocolate ice cream makes you happy." He paused and observed insightfully, "Yes, but not now."

Even a four-year old understands that externally derived happiness is fleeting.

It's well established that sustained happiness is not directly a product of affluence; nor is it derived from sex, power, position, fame or drugs. Happiness is lasting when it comes from tapping into the affirming and elevating power within us and in life. Living empowered by Scend releases us from the destructive effects of struggle. Bad events in life (we can't always dodge or discount them) do not hold us down when we are resolved, self-assured and internally driven. We can remain resilient whatever fate throws against us.

The people we studied who are confident they have attained high spirituality typically say these things: "I feel an expanding sense of being guided from within." "I have inner peace." Yes, and they have a glow because they are at peace with themselves and with life. It's like that lighthearted lilt we all feel when we have gone to the beach on an early summer day.

Are there actions triumphant folks take that translate into Scend-filled living? Our research points to three:

> Doing the disciplined work of getting into position— that is, getting control of spiritual struggle;
>
> Launching ourselves forward through loyalty, belief, empathy, and connection; then, finally,
>
> Letting go, so we are carried forward by a great force — in, around, under, and through us.

Again my thoughts are drawn inexorably to body surfing — riding a giant, exploding mountain of water down the chute into the froth of sand and sea. It's a totally exhilarating experience — in everyday language: it's awesome. You work yourself through the turbulence into the swell until you're in position, ready for launch. When your vault forward is attuned to the wave's releasing power, you are transformed into a quiet-yet-powerful missile, gliding harmlessly into the calm and sinking into head-to-toe relaxation.

Yes, you're jostled here and there, sometimes bruised even bloodied. Small protrusions poke you; sand and shells scrape at your body; the jarring power of the water momentarily alarms you; but the overall experience is—in reality—breathtaking. It's a Scend! Cool water kisses your face, your heart jumps with joy and you exclaim, "More! More!"

That feeling is akin to the contentment with life people we researched say they desire — an afterglow — not just in extraordinary moments (as about half of those we queried report they have experienced though only on rare occasions), but daily –undergirding our every moment.

That's life above destructive struggles.

CHAPTER 4
GETTING IN THE CURL

L IFE ABOVE DESTRUCTIVE STRUGGLE doesn't come naturally, especially since we've been programmed in modern society to think and act quite differently, to say reflexively, "When it rains, it pours." Instead, as we wander life's beaches, what should we do? First and foremost, we have to look for the "right" waves, then position ourselves to be captured by their releasing power and, once set, take courage, and go!

We have to position ourselves to engage in spiritual surfing, to break clear from thrashing about in the waters of life to being propelled upward and forward — as if carried by a great swell, Scend.

It's about getting above struggles that unsettle our relationships — at home, at work, in everyday life, actually and virtually. It's about abandoning our everyday practice of denial. That means it's about not blaming others, bad luck or external forces. In a word, it's about getting drama out of our lives. It's about experiencing spiritual wholeness, purpose, meaning, even fulfillment, all the days of our lives — that's spiritual well-being!

So hopefulness instead of helplessness; positivity instead of negativity; acting like champions instead of being victims.

It's all about being carried forward to remarkable goodness, quiet strength, and enduring satisfaction. That's what we seek. And that's what we can achieve through the spiritual power resident within us when that power is released into our daily lives and the lives of others we touch.

Historically, followers of most religions, particularly those from the Near East (Judaism, Christianity, and Islam) look to the god above the world to get them past their troubles, to provide sanctuary against the forces that overrun them as individuals. These followers believe their struggles can only be quieted supernaturally – all struggles – struggles with partners and coworkers as well as struggles with such issues as body image, addictions, fatigue, debt, poor health, cheats, troublesome neighbors, bullies, rapacious business competitors, and the like. Just listen to their prayer requests. They are mostly focused on these kinds of matters. But here's the rub: too many times, despite fervent prayers and petitions, these struggles run their course exactly as they do for those who utter no such pleas.

"Outside" help, in other words, only arrives occasionally, and more likely than not, in the form of good fortune. Ardent faith commitments, when it's all said and done, do not predictably produce the desired outcomes they often claim. Fate wins out time and again.

To live above the threats and vicissitudes of life requires a very different approach than seeking salvation from the outside. Directly put it's this: Becoming open to self, to the voice within. As it turns out, it's the inside connection that delivers.

My mind turns to the cellar wall of a 1930's house still standing in Cologne, Germany. On it is found this poem apparently scrawled by a Jewish teenager hiding from Nazi oppression:

> ". . . sometimes in this suffering and hopeless despair my heart cries for shelter. But a voice rises within me saying, 'Hold on my child; I'll give you strength, I'll give you hope. Just stay a little while."

What is meant by speaking of a "self" which grants us an inner voice? If we wish to be analytically precise, self is the integration of our genetic and cultural endowments fleshed out by multitudes of personal life experiences. Self develops as we piece together throughout our lives a narrative that weaves into one dramatic cloth our primal past with our many faceted history of experience. It's our genetic stuff shaped by myriads of conscious and subconscious events presented to the world as our persona.

When we act from our inner self, which is, I contend, our authentic self, we take on life each day from inner strength, therefore with confidence and strength. Then we are able to handle successfully whatever comes at us from over the horizon.

As we noted before, although only a small percentage

of adult Americans say they themselves are satisfied spiritually, more than eighty percent recount that they have encountered at least one other person who is "spiritually satisfied." Apparently, most of us know paragons of spirituality, the "saints" among us, but few of us are confident we have found their pathway to spiritual living, this despite powerful religious movements which have captured billions of people around the world.

Take the extraordinary global success of the Holiness Movement in the 21st century. It shows how widespread and magnetic is this interest, yet how perilous the trek. Most Pentecostals are certain they are inspired directly by God's Holy Spirit. Nevertheless, our interviews with many of them have revealed that more times than not they live out roller-coaster lives. Time and again they fall short of expectations (they "sin") causing many, they believe, virtually to lose their salvation. Then come anguished repentance and, sometime later, the assurance God has rescued them yet again — but only to experience a fall once more "from grace" into anguish and despair! This cycle is typically repeated again and again —virtually till death or Alzheimer's, or, in a few cases, when despair or disbelief sets in.

As for more traditional churchgoers, they too strive to increase their spiritual standing though with less zeal. And they, too, invariably report that in doing so they run into powerful headwinds of doubt and failure. They want to imitate Christ. They want to work out their own salvation, even if it produces fear and trembling. But a secure beachhead they seldom achieve. What's missing? Releasing the power of the spirit within — that's what's missing. When we do so, our lives are transformed.

How do we make this happen? Actually, there may well be a number of ways to promote inner, self-driven, Scend-filled living. Our studies through focus groups and survey science reveal that following five specific strategies and recording them in our spiritual muscle memories invariably produces this state of transparent well-being—spirituality.

The strategies build one upon the other, from what is foundational to what finally delivers us to Scend-filled living. And here's the good news, these five life strategies are at work in people from coast to coast and around the world, whatever their gender, ethnicity or station in life.

When we let them guide our daily living, especially when we cobble them together like wires into a powerful cable, they bring us into the releasing power of spiritual waves—to life through Scend.

CHAPTER VI
FACING DANGEROUS WATERS

America is experiencing some decline in religious affiliation these days. Meanwhile, there's a dramatic upsurge in interest in things spiritual. That's what PEW researchers report. The social media paint the same picture. Millions of "friends" tell virtually and continuously of their ventures to grow spiritually. They like to inform us about their connections to others. We get the impression that this is one motivating reason why they are reaching out to a world of virtual sojourners. That's also why they shop religious movements and sometimes follow after spiritual gurus.

Some speak about trying to live out their inner longings. They say they want their lives to be consistent with their deeply embedded values. They wish to have purpose and authenticity dominate their lives. They wish, in the simplest of terms, to be spiritually whole. They want graced lives.

In fact, most everyone wants relationships that are enriching, fulfilling and, certainly, enduring. We strive for personal security, for a world that is fair, a place that is safe for us and our children. We want our spiritual journeys to be well-springs of happiness. For those of us who are Christian, we want to experience every day the healing spirit of Christ: truly loving God, our very selves, and others about us—and feeling the warmth of their love in return.

But here's our dilemma: even those of us who say our spiritual lives are strong, when we are stopped and asked about our immediate situation, we often confess to harboring doubts. And these doubts pull us into struggle. If unchecked, they can lead us to spiritual bankruptcy—death by a thousand fears.

When people fear their spiritual search will come up short, they falter. When this unsettling outlook has "high power" (that is, when skepticism and negativity make sense of a great deal of our world), and when this outlook is easy to confirm (bad things are happening all the time!), a turnaround can't be made. Spiritual struggle ensues, and it's difficult to shake.

So people worldwide—in cities large and small, suburbs, rural areas, yes, even idyllic outposts— all together experience life as though they are swimming in dangerous waters. Life, for them, is struggle. Spiritual well-being—life above destructive struggle— though highly sought after and prized, remains elusive.

Upon reflection, the spiritual search is many times like the quest for the perfect holiday. Usually it doesn't turn out the way the travel agent promised.

I was vacationing in Cancun some winters ago following the lure of warmth and adventure. One morning I set out for Isla Mujeres, a small island off the coast—a skin diver's paradise. I prepared carefully for the boat ride and the day—wearing just a swimsuit, an old T-shirt and thongs, with mask and fins in hand and with a U.S. twenty-dollar bill and some pesos in my back pocket.

Once on the island, while strolling down the beach, I spied a formation jutting out of the water about a hundred yards offshore—an entrancing spot for lunch, I thought. So I bought a sandwich with my pesos, left behind my thongs and shirt, and began my swim to serenity, sandwich arm held high. My plan seemed perfect, but life rarely is that way. What happened next was wild and woolly. As I tired, my "sandwich hand"—without my   realizing it— dropped just beneath the surface of the water and set off total pandemonium below. Fish of all sizes ascended in a virtual feeding frenzy—devouring my food, biting my hand, and sending me into such convulsions that my twenty-dollar bill came loose from my pocket and was torn to pieces as it floated to the surface!

I was in strange waters—as it turned out, perilous ones at that! My well-laid plans didn't take into account the real dangers before me, but, by the best of fortune, my day was saved by honeymooners from Houston who loaned me money for food and the boat ride back to Cancun.

Most people experience life this way—they begin with high hopes and grand plans; and they have some initial success. There is the exhilaration of adventure. But, partway to their destination, they run into "spoilers" that interrupt their plans and strip them of security.

Sometimes, luck is on their side and they are rescued; other times, though perhaps only momentarily, they are sent into convulsive struggle.

Why doesn't God bail them out? Why are they put to the test? When we asked a cross section of people (including devout churchgoers) whether they felt, in that moment, spiritually strong, connected with God and secure, more than two-thirds said, "No." Not surprising! Most faiths recognize that the struggle for spiritual wholeness requires ongoing renewal, continuous touch points to keep followers on course, special ceremonies and retreats to light anew spiritual flames. Yes, we believe; no, we aren't always spiritually connected and empowered. We struggle. And since spiritual struggle, by definition, arises from the core of our being, it can be truly daunting.

My doctorate in philosophy of religion and religious life haven't hardwired me, as I once expected, to spiritual satisfaction. On the contrary, my spiritual pursuit was complicated, not simplified, by study and belief. As is said in popular lore, it's a long trip from the brain to the heart.

Study and belief often put people in tension with those with other world views, and, sometimes, even require believers to distort or deny widely accepted understandings of the world. Study also may bring into focus perplexing conflicts within the scriptures, in theology, in faith, in living. In any case, almost always, the search for truth ends up focused on tradition, therefore on the past, not on our personal daily challenges and opportunities. As a result, spirituality and religiosity don't always come together. Indeed, sometimes, they are contraries!

Religion, especially in the Western world, traditionally reduces spiritual struggle to the workings of others, most often evil powers. The promise of relief, therefore, rests with an intervening God. This is the strength of these traditions; and it is their profound weakness. So there are moments of elation as the faithful celebrate "answers to prayers" and "victories over evil." But then come the moments of confusion and disappointment when God does not respond. The good die from pancreatic cancer in the same percentages and with the same anguish as the bad. Notre Dame and Liberty University football teams win and lose with a frequency that appears to be entirely unrelated to the fervor of the prayers in the locker room before the game and at half-time. Actually, if God did intervene on behalf of the righteous in answer to their pleas, those who wager on sports would be beating a path to these teams!

Here's another dilemma: many religious traditions steer their faithful into conflict with those holding other points of view — scientific, secular, humanistic, to name a few, to say nothing of those representing other religious beliefs and expressions. Because spirituality builds on openness to others, preoccupation with doctrines that define (set limits on) those who are "in" and those who are "out" actually takes seekers away from spiritual living, not to it. This is the reason why ideology and dogma so commonly yield judgment, vilification, even violence—not Christ-like care for others. The long and tortured histories of Judaism, Christianity and Islam make this point with exclamation.

So here is the predicament: the faithful labor to find God's peace; but the more they study, the narrower their world views and the more likely they come into tension with the followers of alternative persuasions. And even more troublesome — as they believe, they find that their beliefs don't speak to everyday struggles, nor do they enable them to find a way out of trouble. Their vision of a hopeful future turns out not to be within their control. So often they drive through life glued to their rearview mirrors, nostalgically committed to the past but unable to relate affirmatively with the new diversity about them.

It is widely recognized that "believers" are not notably freer than others from insincerity, insecurity, inner doubt, insensitivity, pettiness, misconduct, rumormongering, and materialism. They do not live remarkably above the injustices of the world. In fact, many times, it is they who perpetuate them! Put more kindly: We all are flawed, at times quite frail; and we all are vulnerable to random violence and occasional missteps.

Spiritual struggle is blind to religious tradition. It's pervasive! Yet followers of most all traditions agree that spiritual living is consistent with:

* sincerity

*connection with others through forgiveness
and compassion, and

* essential goodness.

This then is the challenge: People have a pretty fair idea
of what spiritual well-being looks like, but this
knowledge doesn't invariably translate into escape
from spiritual struggle. So how do we make this
journey a success? Why are so many folks caught up
in spiritual struggle?

Our research shows that most are pulled by life events
into four debilitating struggles: we struggle with
insecurity; we struggle with injustice; we struggle with
insincerity; and we struggle with inauthenticity. These
struggles, in the language of surfing, wipe us out.

Let's explore each struggle more deeply.

CHAPTER VII
WIPING OUT THROUGH INSECURITY

I WAS SHOCKED BY MY MOTHER'S panic when she was to have a hysterectomy. By everyone's account, she was a saint—a respected Bible teacher, a moral giant, a model of Christian living. My shock came from her response to going under the knife for a significant, but not mortally threatening, procedure. It spoke of a deep insecurity, one I didn't expect from a person who traveled each moment with God. I hadn't realized she lived in profound spiritual struggle. As I discovered, as strong as her faith was, it couldn't carry her through this life event with assurance of recovery. She believed she was in the hands of an all-powerful and loving God who knew her as his special child; nevertheless, she wasn't confident of the outcome.

My mother is not unique. It's common for people of faith to report that they yearn to be close to God, to be at peace—above all, to have inner confidence God is with them—but nevertheless to fall into anxiety. That's often why they hold on to their beliefs with such fervor. But when crisis moments arrive their grip often gives way and they fall into the paralyzing grasp of insecurity.

They assure themselves God will sustain them in their hour of need but, when challenge comes, they are fraught with apprehension. Will God be there when all else has failed? Will he rescue the faithful?

I recall the words of desperation of New York City firefighter Anthony Pasquali the day the World Trade Center towers fell to rubble. A CNN reporter asked about his buddies, most likely caught in the catastrophe. "Hopefully," he sighed, "God is with us." — We now know: God did not rescue them!

Am I painting our lives in too bleak terms? After all, most of us don't awaken every day shackled by anxiety and deep, debilitating insecurity. There are times our struggles with insecurity, in fact, yield positive results. They may even drive us to peak performance. But, with uncommon exception, insecurity tears at us and takes us down. Yes, we have luminous moments. We feel God is with us; things are going right. In those moments we feel strong, confident, empowered. But these occasions are more often than not fleeting, especially when we face financial misfortune, disease, relationship break-up, loss of a job or a friend.

Why do these normal-as-blueberry-pie outbreaks of insecurity keep us from spiritual well-being? I gained a new perspective on anxiety over several clear winter nights in Utah. Some of our anxieties stem from events in our lives years ago.

Every evening for a week, two weary skiers shared with me our resort spa. We related stories of our escapades on the slopes and occasional insights into our everyday lives back home. The second night, we were joined by Margot. She was mostly a non-skier, certainly a non-boarder, who had come to the mountains to escort her teenage son and daughter. By the end of her second sojourn with us, she had changed the focus of our conversations. Margot was in spiritual crisis and she wanted help—from us, safe strangers far from her home locale.

A minister's wife, she felt she had to be a model of spirituality, at least around her husband's parishioners. "I'm called on to counsel women in crisis, young people trying to sort out relationship and sexual issues," she confided, "but I'm not the person they think I am." We focused that evening on the painful difficulty of living up to the unrealistic expectations of others.

The next evening, when Margot took her place in the spa, our discussion quickly moved off the slopes back to her plight. This time, she took us from the struggle of living a sainted life to how base insecurities keep us from spiritual peace. "Whatever the scriptures say," she confided to me, "I don't believe I'm forgiven." "What is it," I asked quietly, "that has so shaken your confidence?"

After a moment of tortured silence, she whispered to me, "When I was twenty, I had an affair with my pastor and had to have an abortion to protect our reputations." She was overcome by grief, though she tried to regain her composure by apologizing for revealing these "terrible things".

I was in a difficult position. Discounting her anxiety

would not suffice. So instead, I offered her some words of comfort mixed with a measure of perspective. We gain little by being haunted by the past, I reflected.

It was Margot's last night on the mountain. She sent a note to me a few weeks later. She felt "a giant weight" had been lifted off of her. She was going to keep her secret in her heart, but her counseling ministry now will reflect more forgiveness.

Perhaps we don't experience the depth of Margot's anxiety, but we may very well carry around burdens from our past — episodes that fuel insecurity. These past crises can rise to consciousness and puncture our canopy of well-being. While reassuring words can at times be heard as hollow, inadequate vessels, unable to blunt the force of destructive events, putting these trials from the past in perspective usually reduces alarm.

So, there are times when we feel elated, exuberant, strong, with a sense that anything is possible; then there are times when we are threatened, unsure about our future, when we say with Lawrence Ferlinghetti, "The world is a beautiful place to be born into, if you don't mind a touch of hell now and then.'"

Insecurity is a key roadblock to sustained spiritual well-being.

CHAPTER VIII
WIPING OUT THROUGH INJUSTICE

ONE MORNING ON THE WAY to work I stopped by Aunt Martha's Pancake House, a not particularly notable breakfast place in one of Chicago's western suburbs. Sitting in a nearby booth was a man who fixed on me with a glaring stare. Finally, he got up and stood over me—menacingly. "Can I help you?" I attempted to get him to back off and reveal his problem. "My cousin used to clean doormats for your college," he barked. "You cut him out. Now, he's hurtin'. If I have my way, you'll hurt too."

I was president of a nearby college, but knew nothing about his cousin's plight. Fortunately, this man never came into my view again, but, that morning, he brought me great discomfort.

We all are subject to unprovoked, irrational assaults, most times not so ominous. Virtually all of us are subject, as well, to the greater injustice of having aches and pains brought on by the countless imperfections of our bodies usually revealed by the passage of time. Many suffer entirely due to unfortunate genetics.

These kinds of "injustices"—random events and built-in failures—bring us to this near-universal recognition:

Too many times what we care about most is at the mercy of what we care the about least.

We care about our personal and family's financial security, so we invest. We care little for those who act selfishly and dishonestly to defraud us of our investments. Unfortunately, we're never sure that our savings aren't at the mercy of a Madoff whose self-aggrandizing conduct can destroy our financial well-being. Wolves in professional clothing can create virtual havoc in our lives by their perfidious deeds!

What's the message? We strive to find a "just" existence, but we are reminded—time and again—that we live in a world short on fairness, no matter how hard we and others strive to make it right. Greed, unrestrained ego, plain old-fashioned jealousy and hatred can make us a casualty of raw injustice. So we struggle.

Rita's bout with injustice came from her workplace affiliation. As spokesperson for her' faculty union local, she stepped into a line of fire she found outrageously unfair.

Rita joined our focus group of high school faculty and staff one afternoon. She was seething with anger and overcome with hurt. She had been singled out at the previous night's public school board meeting by the governing body's chairman for being "more concerned for the advancement of your teacher union than for your students." She was livid and recoiling. With a reputation as an outstanding teacher and with a string of stellar evaluations in her file, she was justifiably angry. "Our world here is monstrously unfair," she erupted. "Little people, like this clueless chairman, want to crush our spirits." She wasn't alone in her feelings. The entire group was dispirited. The chairman's statements had reminded them ruefully that they don't always operate in a just world. When they pressed for salary improvement, they incurred the overreaching wrath of the chairman of the school board. It was for Rita an agonizing time and defining moment.

Our session focused on the real architecture of life, on how our lives often are pierced by injustice, sometimes rudely, and how these ugly interruptions drain our strength and leave us in despair. And we spent some time getting everyone past lamenting this injustice to recognizing that she and her colleagues were the winners. When this man lowered himself by the nature of his attack he elevated them.

We live every day with injustices—the exploitative attack of others upon us (like those of the school board chairman on Rita), the unfair judgments people make of us (like the menacing assertions I heard from a stranger on an otherwise fine day), and the unexpected perils of disease, accident, frailty, natural disaster, violence, even acts of terror. It's not easy to cope with these injustices because they visit us most times without warning, sometimes with cruel force. But we can rise above such struggles.

Yes, injustices have the power to shatter our hopes and

dreams. We know, as James Baldwin observed about racism, that injustice abounds, but we must never accept injustice as commonplace. To take injustice as the norm will certainly propel us into spiritual struggle.

So here's the worst: We care a great deal about living but our lives can be taken in a flash by accident, illness, or a random act of violence. We want to believe, but doubt is present even in moments we believe. We long to be whole, but the loss of a child, of a job, of a relationship, of our own health put us at risk. To protect ourselves, we become guarded, sometimes controlled by suspicion; so we withdraw. After all, every day our fears are reinforced as we are barraged with the misfortunes and misdeeds of others—on the national and local news as well as from the gossip friends relay to us by text or tweet, in the hallway at work, or through our social media friends. It's easy to become tainted by this constant exposure to the seamy side of life as well as the many perplexing uncertainties of life. But when we are wary and negative, we lose our spiritual mooring.

The many and sometimes ugly injustices of the world bring us to spiritual struggle.

CHAPTER IX
WIPING OUT THROUGH INSINCERITY

FOR MORE THAN A QUARTER-CENTURY, I've been at the top of relatively large institutions of higher learning. As I reflect on those years, I see remarkable achievements—organizational and individual. But I also see the treacheries of everyday people in the workplace as they maneuver for power, security, recognition, advancement, retribution. Rarely are these treacheries naked. Those involved may speak kindly to each other, even swear friendship and loyalty. But their blades are long, and they show little hesitation to drive them into the backs of their associates! It's a common observation: There are no more ruthless politics than campus politics.

I received a long letter from a future subordinate a week or so before I began a new job as president of a college. In it, she graciously pledged steadfast loyalty, spoke with admiration, and characterized' my coming to campus as an "extraordinary opportunity for her to learn." She also related certain conspiratorial acts under way to ensure that I had early failures— the acts, of course, of named and unnamed others. I was astonished by the scope and gravity of her revelations but pleased with this gesture of support.

Soon after my arrival, the editor of the local newspaper

shared with me a concern that a high-ranking official of the college had attempted to have the paper publish what his researchers found to be untrue and slanderous reports about me. Who was this person? It was none other than my "loyal" subordinate letter writer!

Of course, I felt betrayed. It took some effort to keep me from suspecting everyone of disingenuous conduct in my new Cabinet.

Insincerity can lead to an insidious form of spiritual struggle; and it's easy to fall into. We live in a world where, every day, people say they care; however, their actions may not conform to' their verbal assurances. Friends say they care, loved ones say they care, colleagues say they care, even strangers say they care. But many images come before us casting doubt upon the sincerity, the potency, and the endurance of these expressions of care.

Words of support when coupled with failure to follow through—no matter what the reason—can bring us to struggle with insincerity. Perhaps those around us mean to act consistently with their assurances; perhaps they don't. The effect is the same. Trust is breached, and breaches of trust strike at the heart of spiritual well-being because they get in the way of open, affirming relationships that are key to effective relations and spiritual health.

We only have to be patients for a short time to recognize that care words can lead to feelings of disappointment, even' betrayal. Practitioners often use these words for encouragement; and sometimes they use them by rote — with little genuine empathy behind them. Families sometimes thrive on these words; other times, they feel violated by them.

My wife developed a close relationship with her physician several years ago. They shared a common interest in Community Theater. When my wife came down with the symptoms of a strep throat while starring in a musical, she called her for help. "I'll do what I can," she was told. "Come in early tomorrow morning." She did, but the examination seemed hurried and incomplete. She did leave with a prescription, but also dismayed. On her way back to the reception area, she noticed her friend's schedule for the day. There her name was — with many others — typed in for "six minutes."

Words of care had been translated, she felt, into minimal care.

These episodes that we all have in life may cause us to doubt the sincerity of those about us—even those committed by profession and relationship to aid us. They often erode our sense of well-being and breed distrust.

Distrust is a seedbed of spiritual malaise.

CHAPTER X
WIPING OUT THROUGH INAUTHENTICITY

THE ULTIMATE SOURCE OF SPIRITUAL struggle comes from a commonly expressed desire to live consistently with our deeply embedded, most cherished ideals.

Most people we spoke with in focus groups said they set out as young adults to make their loftiest hopes and aspirations reality. By midlife, however, they realized how difficult this is to do. Inner struggles set in.

I began to recognize the true proportions of this form of spiritual struggle when I met Jack at a conference of social workers in Southern California some years ago. Jack and I were co-presenters. He appeared to be a "together" man, principled, a model of emotional health.

I was taken aback when he called several months later to seek counsel. He was in struggle. His wasn't a struggle with belief or denominational particulars; it was the kind most of us experience at that point in life when we pause to ask what we're doing, where we're going—and why. As he related, he was caught between a commitment to "be there" for all of his clients and a personal financial crisis. He found himself—for the first time in his career—in the position where he had to turn away clients in real need of his service because they might not meet their fee obligations. Money was beginning to govern his practice. He was conflicted! He felt spiritually adrift.

Jack's struggle was to live out faithfully the convictions that propelled him into the field of counseling years before, convictions which were founded on commitments to care rather than compensation. Put simply: He was repulsed by hypocrisy creeping into his life. He wanted his work to be consistent with his innermost values and aspirations. He wanted, above all, to feel at home with himself—in his work as well as in his private life. He desired the strength that authenticity brings to all of life. Nevertheless, he was damned if he didn't see therapy as a business, and, of course, damned if he did.

This is a prevalent form of spiritual struggle: being caught between two opposing moral choices. As I expected, Jack, an extraordinarily caring and sensitive man, resolved his struggle through a painful restructure of his finances, trading down cars and office space — a difficult but laudable decision.

Like Jack, most people long to carry on their lives in tune with their ideals. They desire reassurance they are on the right path. They seek a vision that will energize them and integrate all of the facets of their lives. But we live in a world where Jack's solution is, many times, against the stream. Most cover their own needs first and rationalize their choices later. Of course, Jack was in a privileged position. He had a choice!

Sometimes resolution is not in our control. Decisions

of others and unforeseen events determine our life course. We know this: we all can be ambushed by jealousy, mean-spiritedness, selfishness, misfortune. We all can be caught up in mega change —economic downturns, office power plays, being in the wrong place at the wrong time, and the like. We all may struggle to live out our ideals.

Inauthenticity blocks us from sustained spiritual well-being. It prevents us from sealing positive relationships with "self" and with others.

So here, in a few words, is why we struggle spiritually. We find it difficult to:

   * break the hold of insecurity
   * cope with injustice
   * reconcile ourselves to a world laced with insincerity; and
   * put our beliefs and values consistently into action.

Generally, we've been taught few effective strategies for getting these things accomplished—and so, only occasionally have we discovered where the power resides that can pull us out of struggle; and only rarely have we used that power.

CHAPTER XI
RIDING THE HEALING WAVES

MAGICAL MOMENTS, ILLUMINATIONS of the human spirit, "soul-to-soul" dialogues with partners, conversations with God, these are not uncommon even in an age of scientific breakthroughs and marketplace dominance. In fact, people speak daily of these experiences. What are their origins? They could be passed off as the products of overactive imagination or undiscerning belief — naiveté. But most people—those who are religious and those who profess no faith—recount them to be bona fide spiritual encounters.

Many years ago, during the Cold War, I interviewed Edward Teller, "the father of the hydrogen bomb," well-known humanist and scientist. I recall his monumental reflection: "I'm certain we (Americans) will prevail (against the Soviets). When you stifle human creativity, the human spirit, you will never match the achievements of those who live and work in freedom."

Clearly, he recognized a spirit that even the most infamous tyrants and crushing systems have not been able to suppress.

In those special moments when we say we are attuned to our inner selves, we are confident we can overcome destructive struggle. We are confident we can get beyond injustice, insincerity, insecurity, even inauthenticity.

Eighty-six percent of our focus group participants agreed that if they live guided by their inner spirit, consistent with their deeply held values and hopes, they will have enduring well-being.

What's such a life look like? How can we keep life struggles from eroding away our spiritual well-being? How can our most wondrous moments be sustained? How can connectedness be nurtured? These are the million-dollar questions we're ready to answer.

Our research reveals that there are several vital life strategies which, if followed and celebrated in our lives, will provide powerful answers to these questions. They will transport us from wallowing in negativity to a bias for optimism, from lonely struggle to healing connections. They will release into our everyday lives the power of Scend.

What are these saving commitments?

CHAPTER XII
STRATEGY ONE: RELATE

S PIRITUAL WELL-BEING, BY DEFINITION, begins in community through healing, empowering, confirming relationships. For some, these bonds are sacramental; for others, they are based on openness and care. Spiritual relationships arise from integrity, out of vulnerability, and through embrace—in a word, from trust. In the language of Jesus, "whoever is least is faithful in that which is most" (Luke 16:10).

Those surveyed who indicated they strongly agreed they were spiritually satisfied consistently scored high on loyalty and fidelity — and they were least likely to say they would give up an important relationship for personal gain, even for a million dollars. They see the integral connection between keeping relationships secure and achieving spiritual well-being. Typically, their "finest expression is to love someone."

It is widely understood that sustained, close relationships are a primary source of happiness—more significant than income, job and social status. They are foundational to spiritual well-being, as well. As early as the second century C.E., Christians recognized that family is where salvation is worked out. Yet, relationships are easily and commonly put at risk, indeed, abandoned entirely. This story has been told in many versions by many people.

Spirituality

Strategy 5: Go forward with Spirit (Inspiration)

Strategy 4: Make the inside connection (Centered Reflection)

Strategy 3: Listen with the Heart (Empathy)

Strategy 2: Respond to the Quiet Voice Within (Belief)

Strategy 1: Build Authentic Relationships (Trust)

I

had lunch with Stuart, a prominent executive known for his business acumen and great marriage. We spoke of common interests, mainly of our diets and wellness plans. As the check arrived and we disputed who would pick it up, a sudden, momentary expression of hurt contorted his otherwise relaxed countenance. "Let's stay here a minute longer," I insisted. "I don't think you're ready to leave. You need to tell me what's going on in your life." He did! Known to virtually no one in the community, he had just received final divorce papers.

Somewhat embarrassed, he revealed that his very comfortable marriage of seventeen years had gone from happy and secure to total disintegration in a matter of months. He pleaded with her to stay, he confided, but that was not to be. She had told their therapist in a final joint session, "I want to start over again. There's no sense in talking further."

My mind flashed back to a party at their home several months before. It had been my most recent encounter with them as a couple. I recall her eyes as she and Stuart danced in the living room—darting about with enticement and sexual energy. I wondered then, "What does it mean?" I know now she was not, as he apparently supposed, settled in to life with him—all other appearances aside.

Of course, loyalty, integrity and honesty are not, in the actual practice of life, so easily charted. Among the questions asked of applicants to highly selective colleges and universities are questions like these: Do you have integrity? Are you honest? Of course, the interviewers are not seeking yes or no answers. They want to determine whether the potential student is trustworthy—and sees the ambiguities that are involved.

There are many possible ways to satisfy these questioners that you have integrity and see the complexities of life. You could impress them by saying that you don't spend money easily because you are faithful both to the provider of your funds and to your own commitment to be prudent. You could assure them that you are honest, except in extraordinary cases when being entirely honest could lead to a greater moral failure — the wrongful taking of a life, the persecution of innocent people, etc. You could tell them you realize integrity is stronger once tested—when it comes out of the crucible of life.

There are ambiguities and complexities in all relationships but, almost universally, people hold loyalty to be foundational to the virtuous life. Of course, living in a complex world can test anyone's resolve to speak and act consistently from trust. And there are times when fidelity is powerfully challenged through life-defining events.

Most people come to a fork in the road at some point in life where they are tested. My turn came on a cold day in the Windy City when I became president of a college in Chicagoland. Not long after I assumed office, I began a campaign of campus beautification. First on the agenda was painting the exteriors of several buildings. Bids were received from local contractors and the "lowest and best" was awarded the contract. To my surprise and consternation, the only work that was completed was the application of a thin coat of paint on the peeling, blistered surface of the administration building.

Sufficiently agitated, I called the contractor myself. His response astonished me. It was entirely beyond any I'd ever heard. "No," he growled, "I'm not going to paint the buildings your way, because then you wouldn't hire me next year to paint them again." He had a nice deal! He could be the annual low bidder, assuring him of the job in perpetuity; and he could carry most of our payment dollars straight to his bank account.

My sharp and immediate response apparently took him off guard. "No," I insisted, "paint the buildings according to our specs or no money!" He paused as if speechless and then thundered: "You'll pay for this!"

Later, I was told this man was a kingpin of organized crime, and that, most likely, my life was in danger—a chilling revelation. But I felt I had no choice. Bowing to his demand would shatter me as a moral person; it was out of the question. In time, we retained another contractor and the buildings were painted. Fortunately, I never heard again from the first contractor. I was confident I had done what was right, not for any other reason, but in its own right.

Acting as though invulnerable, doing what is right despite evident risk, brings us in touch with our inner strength and positions us to act with integrity in all our dealings.

There also are times when relationships are secured through vulnerability. Being vulnerable to those who are close actually builds intuitive bonds. But it isn't easy. Research psychologists have found that a single negative experience with a friend or partner will, almost invariably, begin to unravel positive feelings we've received from many affirming interactions. In short, we as humans are predisposed against vulnerability. In fact, we hate being vulnerable.

Over millennia, humans have survived by giving bad events far more weight than good ones, and for good reason. Seeing all opportunities as potentially enhancing can lead to disaster. Some may very well end up being destructive. So, most of us, by nature, are wary of letting others see our soft side. We strive to be—or, at least, to appear—invulnerable, even to ourselves.

Nevertheless, here's what our research shows: those who take measured risks and reach out to others in openness are more likely to experience spiritual well-being, especially those who take the even greater risk of finding and living from their authentic selves.

The stories told in this book usually are about extraordinary happenings and exceptional people doing exceptional things—the "best of the best." Here garden-variety accounts make the point. The vulnerability upon which spiritual life is built is expressed customarily in small gestures, "random acts of kindness"—like the opening of flowers in a meadow at daybreak. A guy revealing to his girlfriend that he has been an alcoholic and is still quite fragile— not the strong man she thinks he is; a neighbor lady who blows snow off the sidewalk in the winter for an elderly man because she cares; a caseworker reporting to her clinic to extend care with a face distorted by Bell's Palsy; all those who risk rejection and undermine their carefully crafted images to support friends — all those "common folks" who reach out in vulnerability to do selfless acts for the betterment of others.

Relationships and trust are remarkably built and sustained when people go against their fears and are open (though not defenseless) to partners in life (friends, mates, parents, children, associates). Certainly, we've suffered disappointment, even disillusionment; and we may have had to close down at some point for our own safety and sanity. Healthy, sustaining relationships, however, come through bonding — especially with those who frame our existence—indeed, with all those whose lives meaningfully intersect ours.

Most of us get the message some time in life that we need to connect. We are, after all, social animals. We need confirmation, support and enrichment from others as well as connection. Even in the Texas Hill Country, where highly successful individualistic people have moved to live sequestered on ranches tens to thousands of acres in size, most everyone there has found it necessary to seek out "neighbors" to solve problems of water supply, traffic congestion, and degradation of the landscape, youth violence, light pollution, and the like. They have bonded with those about them through churches and political movements. And as they have, they have found purpose and social power.

Typically, we travel in the opposite direction, trapped in lifestyles that strengthen connections with "virtual friends" (who may actually just be "Catfish" friends), but weaken connections both with those directly about us and with our local community. We drive encased in our cars, usually alone; we text and tweet with sojourners far from us more often than those nearby; we work out of closed spaces —offices and cubicles; we hold neighbors at bay by walls, fences and dogs; and we hang out with most others at a distance — via mobile devices, using FB, text messaging, etc.

It's now the norm to move away from family, watch TV alone, play games solo on our iPads and mobile devices, exercise in isolation; shop by eBay and Amazon; and study online.

Who we are in relation to others is not so much personal as much as it is commercial. This is why so many are lonely, some even futureless including many of our most affluent and otherwise successful citizens.

This is quite different from the cultures of our parents and ancestors. I got some insight into this when traveling some years ago through a small town in southern Italy on the way to view the remnants of a 2nd century B.C. Greek temple. We passed by two men sitting on a wall next to the roadway. I took special note of them because they were face-to-face, virtually a few inches apart, apparently consumed by friendly conversation. About two hours later we came back past the same location — and there they were, as before, face-to-face, with pleasing countenance, totally absorbed in their conversation. How different is our world!

Our research shows that separation from others is not conducive to emotional and spiritual health. It leads us into struggles including the struggle with inauthenticity. Worse, we as individuals can slip from isolation to alienation — self-defeating estrangement from others and from ourselves.

Loneliness can be hurtful; alienation is often debilitating.

When does this slide occur? A story from our legendary past clarifies how. Years ago, the collector of *The Jack Tales*, folklorist Richard Chase, my companion on a train ride from Los Angeles to Santa Barbara, led me beyond the beanstalk saga of our childhood into Jack's doings in the mountains of Carolina and, more important, to an uncommon insight into the common experience we often call "alienation" (the root of inauthenticity).

Jack was a young farmer, the writer noted. He was

moving west with his kin into the foothills. They were clearing "new ground" so that they could extend their land and make a better living. This very understandable and peaceful journey brought them into direct confrontation with backwoods people, very different folks!

In the story, Chase relates, the people Jack and his brothers encounter actually came from the same English stock; but they had forged an entirely different culture based on mountain living. To Jack, they were strangers; soon they were adversaries. They couldn't be trusted and certainly not befriended. Some were, as he imagined, ruthless and savage — two-headed giants!

As the Jack's tales unfold, we learn more about his deep fear of these "monsters of the forest." We learn that Jack was anxiety-ridden because he didn't feel safe with the people up the road. He was in their world; and he wasn't wanted in their world. In fact, his new-found enemies were determined to get rid of him and his brothers. And so, as the stories go, he schemed to get rid of them.

When we reduce these tales from myth to reality, we realize that Jack had slipped from the dread of feeling isolated in a new locale, to the full-blown alienation of being in a foreign land among hostile strangers. He had lost his moorings and soon, his sense of self. Of course, though not at all recognized in the book, his backwoods adversaries felt the very same way. After all, it was their world that the intruders—Jack and his brothers—had entered intent upon changing.

As Jack and his kin—and his adversaries—experienced, their foundations were shifting. They didn't feel "at home"—safe—any longer. They were in a dangerous world; they were displaced persons; as such, they were powerless. That is alienation—separation from all things familiar that grant us security and authenticity resulting in a crippling feeling of apprehension—angst.

There are people today, like Jack and his brothers, who come and cut in our forest; they make our backyards unfamiliar worlds. They may even bring us to social bankruptcy, as if we've been relocated to a strange land. When intruders come into our lives who, we suspect, are not operating with our well-being in mind, we begin to experience not only separation from others and from familiar places, but separation from our very selves.

To salvage meaning and purpose, many put their life's energy into climbing up the power/security ladder, buying houses of greater size, achieving envied lifestyles. But, commonly, when these aspirations are reached, they are no more secure, no more in tune with themselves, no more satisfied than they were before. Their search is inadequate to the task of overcoming the dread of alienation!

The pathway to security is commonly experienced as circuitous and difficult to follow. In fact, it may be quite simple to follow. I love this Buddha story:

One day, Buddha, so the story goes, came across an

ascetic, presumably a monk, who had practiced a very austere, self-denying lifestyle for years. The Buddha asked him, "What did you get for all your effort and sacrifice?" Proudly, the ascetic replied, "Now I can cross the river by walking on the water. The Buddha was not impressed. He pointed out that self-denial had yielded very little. "I, too, can cross the river," he admonished, "by ferry and for just one penny."

What's the lesson? We can go far out of our way to achieve a prized goal, but our efforts may take us no farther than what is available to us already. The simple way to cross the river may well be available readily: reaching out to embrace those who intersect our life paths, not treating them without careful reflection as strangers and adversaries.

The first five years after September 11, 2001, according to the National Opinion Research Center, the percentage of people who "feel others are helpful" was on a sharp trend line up. That percentage sunk back to pre-9/11 levels by the disaster's tenth anniversary; and it has remained low ever since. Regrettable! Reaching out and building relationships based on transparency and vulnerability—connecting even with "intruders"— keeps people from alienation, grants them inner strength, and frees them from spiritual struggle.

How can we do this? We do this by looking past judging to accepting, and by giving up dominating for embracing. When people reach out to others about them they find peace with themselves. If Jack and his brothers had taken apple pies up the road to their new neighbors instead of brandishing axes, they would have affirmed who they were and avoided needless struggle; and they would have escaped alienation.

The modern world is hard-edged, patched together by cold words: the words of legal contracts, the words of our employers' policies and procedures, the words of clichés and empty greetings, even words that are "little white lies." Taking cold words and turning them into warm words—words of care and concern—overcomes alienation, from others and from self.

Strong relationships — face-to-face as well as virtual — keep us from sliding into alienation and inauthenticity and, thus, into spiritual struggle. Those who remain committed to their family, their community of faith, their neighbors and friends, those who work for reconciliation, and those who reach out even to those pulling away, tranScend the abyss of separation. They are on the right road — from alienation to spiritual well-being.

CHAPTER XIII

STRATEGY TWO: RESPOND

SO OFTEN, GIVEN THE EXPLOSION OF religious sects and the virtual omnipresence of televangelists and their ilk, when people search for meaning, connectedness, freedom from struggle, and significance, they often end up under the spell of a compelling personality or cultic belief. They seek "truth" and truth tellers who can stand the challenges of cynicism and the grit in everyday living.

When we scan the spiritual landscape, however, we discover that enduring spiritual strength rarely comes through the teachings of such charismatic religious leaders. The common ups and downs of their converts bear vivid testimony to this fact.

The founders and prophets of the world's great religions, in fact, were likely not spellbinders. They were ordinary people who responded powerfully to a compelling voice from within: the nomad Abraham; the illiterate Muhammad; the peasant girl in Bethlehem, Mary; the lowly carpenter, Jesus; the voluntarily impoverished Buddha. And in each faith tradition, through sacred writings, worship, singing, praying or meditating, celebrating sacraments, ordinary people hear the voice within and become spiritually whole.

The everyday illuminations that are central to spiritual

life invariably come from within. This is consistent with the recent findings of scientists that the deepest origins of religion are based in mystical experience as well as with St. Paul's observation that "with the heart one believes unto righteousness" (Romans 10:10).

Mystical experience appears to have been formative to the world's major religious traditions — found in larger doses in Hinduism, Buddhism, and Taoism, as well as a well-recognized stream (though sometimes subterranean and oftentimes disturbing) of Judaism, Christianity and Islam.

The need to purge oneself of the contamination of the world and suspend faculties, though common, is not what I am referring to. What I am speaking of is union with self and thus the Transcendent. This experience takes form in Christianity based on Jesus' vision described in the Gospel of John. It is of his spiritual union with followers after his return (see chapters 14-17). The Pauline epistles are laced with references to the Apostle's desire to be one — personally and profoundly — with Christ. Christian mystical experience is not necessarily ecstatic or revelatory; it attempts to discern the "Beyond" that is "Within."

Leaders of virtually all of the world's religious traditions teach that God is heard through people's inner selves — their souls. Stories of faith resonate "in the heart"; followers are moved by ceremony to well up inside; believers stand in awe of God's magnificent expressions in nature; and so often, God, they believe, responds to their prayers through that "quiet voice within."

The faithful seek healing in Christianity (salvation), wisdom in Buddhism (enlightenment), liberation from the cycle of misery in Hinduism (nirvana), oneness with God and his people in Judaism (sanctification), conformity to the will of God in Islam (submission)— all granted, not as thunderbolts from another world, but as revelations from within. Sometimes, these revelations are translated through religious leaders, sometimes through those outside religious traditions, even, at times, through the profane.

I had just moved to Ohio. It was April Fool's Day, but, no fooling, it was bleak and cold. We decided against cabin fever and made our way to the restaurant guide's "best-spot." When we arrived we found a party in progress. To our delight, we were included — immediately! Our host was Tom, a local car dealer—a deal-maker supreme, earthy, somewhat rough around the edges, but altogether winsome, even inspiring.

As we became friends, I discovered the real Tom. When our mutual friend, a banker, was in his last months of fighting against a fatal cancer, Tom called him each morning at 8:00 a.m. to raise his spirits for the difficult day ahead.

Tom wasn't a theologian; he wasn't an elder in a church; he wasn't even a church member. But, as he related to me when our friend passed on, he had an inner prodding to reach out to our dying friend. It gave to him — certainly also our banker friend — a strong sense of contentment.

People we surveyed, no matter what faith commitment, consistently reported that when they listened to the voice within, gnawing emptiness dissolved; a sense of well-being was theirs. Heeding the voice inside bestowed on them both emotional and spiritual security.

We can conclude this: if people reorder their spiritual lives—from a search for messages from a god outside to openness to the constant God Within—they will surge forward to experience a healing sense of serenity.

St. Augustine captured this essential principle nearly seventeen centuries ago when he wrote:

"And what place is there...in me into which my God can come, even He who made heaven and earth? Is there anything in me, O Lord my God that can contain Thee? In Thee, from whom are all things, by whom are all things, in whom...are all things?"

Beliefs didn't drive Tom to exemplary acts of kindness; nor did he receive messages from an outside power directing him to intervene. Inner conviction spurred him to action.

In our everyday parlance we use the word "belief" to mean doctrine, dogma, some specific set of "truths." That's because we've been influenced by the modern world of science to think beliefs have to be facts. As it turns out, "belief"—traditionally and fundamentally— is something quite different. It's simply expressing faith; it's embracing others in trust. Beliefs as facts drive people apart. Belief as faith brings folks together. Beliefs as facts take us to the head. Belief as faith comes from the heart! That's why it's very difficult to get agreement on what's "true." After all, no two people tell a story, see the world precisely the same way.

Better to be led from within.

How can we describe this experience? As having a strong intuitive sense of direction, as feeling a whoosh of effortless achievement, as cutting through resistance like a warm knife through butter, as building a toned and muscular spiritual disposition, as realizing a peace which passes understanding? Actually, as all of the above!

Being led from within also streamlines life.

How does this occur? Patti revealed "Step One" when she spoke out in a focus group held just after the first of the year. Our discussion had centered on our New Year's resolutions and our usually poor record of achieving them. She turned the conversation on end with this surprising pronouncement: "Here's my resolution:—I'm going to do less each day this year until I get to the point where only essential things get done!"

Exactly what does she intend to jettison? "All meetings where my presence makes no real difference; all trips to malls and stores for things I'll probably end up putting away or giving to charity; all chores that are not needed for the family's health and happiness; all frivolous tweeting and Facebooking, certainly mind-numbing TV-watching — everything I do that doesn't take me directly to where I want to go; everything I do that isn't truly enriching for me, my family and others."

Patti is off and running — and in the right direction. She is streamlining!

When we reduce our many pursuits down to centering on the primary everyday goal of spiritual well-being, a key lifestyle change has occurred. And, when this life reorientation is made habitual, we will experience a new level of living. Specifically, we will separate what wins the day from what occupies time. We will get a new perspective on life and become willing to become less.

How can this life reorientation occur when we're overwhelmed by a tsunami of responsibilities and obligations? We have to follow Patti's lead and commit to streamlining.

In the water, streamlining is pushing off a solid poolside, stretching out, reaching arms and hands as one toward our destination, and gliding as far as initial breath and thrust can carry us. With such a smooth and powerful start, competitive swimmers launch themselves effortlessly and gracefully.

In the spiritual domain, streamlining is pushing off from a firm foundation—our deeply embedded values, our fundamental sense of who we are. Goal-directed, having clear purpose in life, remaining confident and under control — no thrashing about because streamlining eliminates unnecessary strokes — we minimize the fear and anxiety that wreak havoc. In a word, we let spiritual streamlining simplify our living.

The prerequisites to streamlining—in both swimming and spirituality—are the same:

*Knowing where we need to go and heading there directly

*Pushing off strong with the confidence we will reach our destination

*Using effective and economical strokes that reduce resistance and exertion

*Gliding along — as if on a great wave — through Scend.

In life, we have to do one thing more to reach our desired destination efficiently. We have to get perspective. We have to understand what is of greatest importance.

Several years ago I hosted a television special featuring several respected enviro-journalists including Mark Schleifstein of the *New Orleans Times-Picayune*. He told about his struggle to get published what became a Pulitzer prize-winning story. It was about oceans on the verge of eco-collapse. His publisher wasn't convinced it should go to print. He could see nothing compelling in the piece, Mark recounted, until he was told that his favorite restaurant, the famous Commanders Palace, will likely soon be out of his favorite fish, red fish, perhaps forever. "Print the story," exclaimed the publisher.

Each of us initially sees our own world, not the world, because our ears and eyes have filters and lenses. When anxieties arise, invariably distortion increases. So when we become confused and frightened by changing landscapes, we tend to close our minds and clutch tenaciously to simplified explanations of life—especially religious explanations in ideological form.

Unfortunately, these pat explanations that lead people to feel sure they are right block connections with others about them, taking away perspective on what actually is right. Typically, as they say in the South, when folks get crosswise with others, they don't socialize together—at least not for long. Knowing this, most ideologues watch pre-selected TV channels, listen to car radio that speaks their language of life—their politics and their prejudices; and they block Facebook and other social media messages that suggest other perspectives, ultimately shunning those who hold those views. Some even burn bridges and abandon long-time friends.

Why are so many convinced they are in the right? Perhaps it's because they've had a riveting experience or been entranced by a consuming personality, a celebrity, a televangelist, a persuasive politician.

Most often, it's because "truths" do some very important things for us:

> *They give us standing;
> *They justify our behavior, past and present, our

lifestyle, especially our prized views;

 *They take the gray issues in life and make them black and white.

*They unravel the mystery of who are the bad guys and who are the good guys.

*Finally and hugely, they put us in an elite group — "the children of the truth"!

It's intoxicating to know you're part of the selected family of the truth. Unfortunately, "truths"—including religious truths—lead away from spirituality because they block out messages from within and, often, they block us from what is actually right. As the old saying goes, the more adamant a person is that he is right, the more likely it is he is not.

Here's what we do know.   Truth doesn't need adamancy.   It can stand on its own feet.   Table thumping, dogmatism and spiritual health don't go well together.

These assertions become obvious when we have the luxury to look back to those before us or those who are at a distance. Few would deny that well-meaning "truth bearers"—no, "truth hurlers"—have used class, gender, race, and belief to mistreat and suppress others, from the Inquisition to slavery to modern genocides and terrorism. And few would deny that it has become increasingly difficult to reach out to others in a world in which religious markers of identity are among the most divisive of all. In any case, it's more difficult to view the prisons of our own minds than the prisons of the minds of those about us.

I found myself at a business lunch several years ago with Harold, the owner of a small manufacturing company. He had just returned from a church conference on "How to Bring Christian Principles into the Workplace." Our conversation held my total attention. His was an amazing story to me, because Harold prides himself on being a spiritual leader.

For twenty-two years, Harold had employed Richard—most recently as his Executive Vice President — a man who, he related, had taken his business from less than $100,000 in annual sales to more than $100 million. "He has made me a rich man," Harold confided, "but I had to let him go this morning. It was the hardest decision I've ever had to make." "I'm sure it was," I reflected, "but why?" His response was immediate and unqualified: "I can't have a shop pleasing to God run by a man like Richard." "What did he do?" I inquired with eager anticipation. "I've warned him for a year," he continued. "His son is an embarrassment to him and to our company. Now, he heads up a gay rights organization. Gays and God don't mix!"

My mind was racing and my heart heavy as I reflected on what this man was telling me. Who knows how great the harm to Richard and his family that will result from this extraordinarily precipitous and overreaching action! Who knows the fear that workers in his plant will feel when they hear about the owner's callous act!

I began the process of exposing the destructiveness of my lunch partner's closed-minded decision—not so much to Richard or to the business—but to Harold himself. To be right spiritually, he committed a terrible spiritual wrong. What an irony! Unfortunately, I didn't get far.

Closed minds and rank prejudice not only prevent bonding with others, they lead otherwise good people to act deplorably, to demonize those with different world views and lifestyles, and tune out the God who is trying to speak to their hearts. Ultimately, they render legitimate beliefs illegitimate and narrow the circle of those they trust and consider as friends and associates. With closed minds, people actually want their news, sermons, political rhetoric, even college lectures to confirm their established views of the world rather than provide new insights.

Closed minds assure us we're right, but at the expense of healing relationships that make us right.

While religious leaders for generations have issued strong admonitions against closed-minded judgment of others—lest one be judged, lest one attempt to avoid self-examination, lest one escape remorse, lest one set oneself up as God—narrow minded believers have projected themselves routinely as the ultimate judges of who is in and who is out, bound for heaven or discharged to hell! Movements within Islam, Judaism, and Christianity—for centuries and in this hour—provide dramatic testimonials to this assertion.

So here is a test to discover whether we have fallen prey to destructive bias:

> *Have our beliefs closed off opportunity for being spontaneous and candid with others who have come into our lives?

> *Will the choices we make today bring us closer to others or separate us from them?

> *How will they appear a year from now— noble or prejudicial?

Those who truly seek spiritual well-being must work to be free of distorting bias. They need to seek out stories of inspiration; they look for works of edification; they reflect on noble lives; they contemplate nature's grandeur and power; and they celebrate great human expressions—through the arts, young children, acts of kindness, ennobling literature, exemplary conduct, and reaching out to others in need. Above all, they give up the very real pleasure of being self-righteous.

CHAPTER XIV
STRATEGY THREE: LISTEN

AMERICA HAS BECOME A NATION OF great diversity. This is fast becoming a trite statement. Poll after poll, census after census reveal that most every city and town from sea to sea has undergone sweeping demographic change in recent decades. Diversity in national origin, race, political persuasion, economic strength—certainly religion—now separates our experience of community from that of past generations. Sometimes we Americans celebrate this newfound pluralism; but most times we respond by insulating ourselves from neighbors and fellow citizens, holding ourselves back from spiritual growth, putting us into spiritual struggle.

Believers speak, especially in church, of love and respect for neighbors, but so often they relate only to the look-alikes around them. Hard to deny: Sundays are the most divisive days in the land.

It's difficult to bridge the gap between ethnic groups and cultures when we live cloistered lives. Right after the Second World War, there was a nearly universal expectation that all peoples and nations would work together for humanity's good and, in the United States, that all Americans would achieve social equity. It was widely expected that religious people of all traditions would find common ground and work together to rid the country, even the planet, of sectarian violence and persecution. The ecumenical movement was well under way. But the century ended with ethnic strife on every continent and with great lifestyle disparities. And in America, there were more factions, not fewer.

In our new century, diabolical acts of terrorism and persistent, embittered regional and ideological conflicts have dashed remaining hopes for peace and unity, internationally as well as in the United States.

How can individuals bond with those like and unlike about them? Not through a common set of beliefs— that is unlikely—but by empathy. Empathy is the miracle potion! It draws others in. It is the catalyst that enables people of all backgrounds to form care communities, communities that enrich our common experience and expand all spirits.

A few years ago, I watched my granddaughter play softball: two teams of ten, in different-colored uniforms, from separate parts of town, all five or six years old, all happy to be together. They came to have fun, but it wasn't long before parents' comments were in the air, revealing other agendas: winning, making certain their "prospect" was given the proper chance to show her stuff, getting the correct stance and swing down pat. You've been there! You've felt the tension, at least your children have!

By inning two, cross-team parent conversations had all but ceased. Camaraderie—all twenty girls enjoying a Saturday morning together, learning what it means to be on a team, gaining a playing skill here and there—had gone by the boards. By the game's end, some were jubilant, others despondent.

Surely, 'I conjectured to myself, fostering empathy would have led to a different outcome. We could bring all parents and players together before each game to meet each other, hear about the other Suzies on the field and focus on our mutual hope: that all the girls would enjoy the experience, take away valuable lessons of teamwork and playing—and be friends; and that all parents would appreciate and encourage all the players. We could have built strong bonds. And we all could have had a more pleasurable Saturday morning!

In the larger world, when communities of care are formed, forces of alienation that pull people into spiritual struggle are neutralized. Caregivers reach out to others, no matter how different they may be; they build intimate affiliations so all can enter—as they say of Chicago's Wrigley Field, the "Friendly Confines" where we know "whose side we're on because we're all on the same side."

Put simply: the catalyst for bonding is empathy. For some, empathy comes naturally. Others less empathic have to follow the lead of actors who seek the truth of the characters they play by studying their words and movements, feeling their emotions, taking them on as the actors' own including their life perspectives and longings. Many rehearsals are required to make the shift from their egos to their characters' egos. So it is with bonding with others through empathy. It takes the special effort of setting aside one's own interests for those of another until empathic behavior is second nature.

What happened on September 11, 2001, reveals that most people are capable of such altruistic conduct. New York City's police and fire services amazed the world with their unrestrained commitment that day and in the months that followed.

Empathy begins with mimicking but it triumphs through compassion—getting inside the skin of others to fathom their needs and hopes, share their struggles, feel their hurts, hear their cry for dignity, and then act accordingly.

Some time ago, I was visiting a former student in Philadelphia who was then attending the Wharton School. Mike and his wife, Stacy, were waiting at the airport when I arrived late at night. On our way to their home, his old Volvo station wagon ran out of gas. It was near midnight. We were marooned in the inner city. Confidently, Mike proposed: "Stay in the car with Stacy. I'll find help. I think there's a bar a block or so up the street. I can hear noise coming from it." Off he went. When he returned, it was with a rough looking, somewhat inebriated man in a coonskin coat who assured us that he would take Mike to find gas and return shortly. Actually, I had thoughts we'd never see Mike again.

After long, anxious moments, they did return—and

with gas. When our stranger-rescuer had fueled the car, I stepped out and offered, "Here's $50 to cover your time and for being so good to us." His response shamed me. "I didn't do this for money," he protested. Then he came close and embraced me. What a lesson!

This man truly displayed extraordinary compassion. I had placed a price tag on his magnanimous act. He nevertheless identified with our plight and saw us as part of his community.

Empathy opens us to others; it also will keep us from hurting others. While I was in graduate school, I pastored a small church nestled in the hills of Pomona, California. The congregation was white; the surrounding neighbors were mostly African American and Hispanic. My assignment was to bring those about us into the fold.

Transformation of the property was step one. The great front landscape of the church soon was populated by slides and swings and a volleyball court, then scores of local children. The sign told more of welcome than of sermons of exclusion, so it was changed. We had become the community center.

I was sitting atop our highest monkey bar one day, surveying the change and enjoying the laughter and delight of the kids who had stopped by. A little African American girl caught my attention. She waved goodbye as she set off for home across a neighbor's front yard. I was appalled to see an elderly white woman burst from her home and begin to strike the child with a broom amidst a hail of racial epithets.

The hurt I experienced was like the hurt of seeing my own child assaulted mindlessly. A glimpse of the African American experience—actually for the first time in my life—became mine. The church grew; our neighbors became our congregation.

Empathy is the healing agent that connects very different people as soul mates. It steels us against fear and misdeeds. Living through empathy is essential to overcoming the spiritual struggles of insecurity, insincerity, and certainly inauthenticity.

What keeps people from empathy? Surely one obstacle is loss and the resulting anxiety of vulnerability. When we suffer loss, we instinctively withdraw from others. We listen through our fears, not with our hearts.

We all experience loss as we make our way through life — loss of opportunity, loss of a loved one, loss of status, loss of power and control, loss of feeling, as we did as teenagers, invulnerable. All of these losses are weakening; some are debilitating. Unchecked, they prevent otherwise strong people from breaking free of struggle. In fact, they deepen our struggles with insecurity, insincerity and injustice.

Loss can be a psycho-spiritual destroyer because its effects are often difficult to shake. It can hold people captive in past pain keeping them from being at peace with themselves.

Loss often is compounded by guilt. "I didn't do enough for my loved one who has passed." "I didn't resolve issues before our separation." "I didn't tell him something very important—I love him." "I should have paid more attention to what he was saying before he committed suicide."

Loss brings us face to face with the inherent injustices of the world. Loss also brings unsettling change; it reminds even the most devout among us that we are ultimately not in control. Loss—even relatively inconsequential loss—rudely calls to mind our own mortality. Loss informs us that what is supposed to be may not be. We are "supposed" to live safely and enjoy a long life. Loss tells us it may be otherwise. Most telling, loss often prevents us from reaching out to others.

When it's all said and done, loss immobilizes—loss of a loved one due to abandonment, divorce, death, or lifestyle; loss of a job; loss of good health! Usually, these losses ambush us; they catch us off guard. Even on the occasions when we know loss is coming (as in the case of a loved one with a terminal illness) or when there's been preparation for years (like the death of a parent), a feeling of being out of control, injured, isolated, and attacked is triggered.

Of course, each of us reacts differently to loss, depending on how involved we have been with the person or thing lost, or our history with losses. Reactions are individualized but, in so many ways, they are similar. Virtually everyone feels betrayed, violated, wary, and anxious— no matter the circumstance. And when we feel betrayed, we no longer listen with our heart. Instead, our focus is on our fears.

A number of observers have identified therapeutic "stages" that people undergo when they suffer profound loss: denial, anger, bargaining, depression, acceptance, and, finally, forbearance. Some think these stages come one after another and in this order. Others believe mourners pass in and out of them. Perhaps one can never get completely free of any of these responses to significant loss.

Grief can't be entirely extinguished. As it is integrated into our lives we increasingly experience a sense of recovery, soon moments of palpable well-being.

The challenge is how to do it. Actor Vincent Price, a longtime friend, taught me one way. For most of life, especially young life, he used to say, we are in the process of building connections and, in so doing, defining and redefining ourselves. Through this process, we flesh out who we are and discover a larger meaning to our lives, even fashion for ourselves a greater self.

Each loss— whether small or catastrophic, whether by divorce, estrangement, relocation, career interruption, or death—therefore represents a stripping away of a piece of our constructed self. The first major loss usually is the most telling because it reverses the building process—and often it's unexpected. It shouts the last thing we want to hear: that we're starting down the back side of the hill of life. The death of my father was my first telling loss. I went from having a strong, resourceful parent who could command away adversity to having a dependent child to having a wilting void to no father at all — forever!

So the first consequential loss begins the process of undoing years of framing and building. If we don't arrest the slide, by old age, we'll become shells. This may be a natural process through which we ready ourselves for our own demise, but it feels outrageously unnatural to me! It cramps the soul and keeps us in spiritual struggle.

I recall Vincent's anguish that so many of his friends were no longer in the entertainment section of the paper; they were in the obituaries. He felt diminished. He was diminished!

Loss is made manageable when it is replaced with gain. Instead of denying loss or trying vainly to let go, new relationships have to replace the old. Certainly, special relationships can't be fully replaced. But the space they vacate in our hearts and minds as they recede from active memory may be filled by new and different attachments.

A focus group of senior citizens in California made this clear to me. I think back especially to one participant, Edgar. He had apparent security and good health in his first years of retirement; and he had a good marriage. Nevertheless, (it made no sense!) he attempted suicide. He drove his car onto a railroad track to end his anguish. Why? What anguish? He felt alone, empty, he revealed to me. He had been a chief engineer in a large corporation; now he did household chores and played golf with buddies. He had been a civic leader; now he added one more body to weekly Kiwanis Club meetings. Nothing he did assuaged his overwhelming sense of meaninglessness. Edgar was in full struggle with inauthenticity. After the train struck his car, he was sent unconscious, to the hospital, but he survived. Through the hospital ordeal, he confided, "I came to realize that I could become a new Edgar." How?

Each day, Edgar sought out a new friend or found someone in need and provided a personal touch of assistance. When he was back to strength, he helped a new florist set up her business; he served as a tutor in English for Mexican immigrants; and he volunteered as an aide for a city councilman. He now has, he told me with a broad smile, "a zest for life and a feeling in my soul that 'all is well.'"

Yes, relatives and friends fall away and we may grieve their loss. But these losses can be made up "by my many gains." Where do these gains come from? They come from listening with the heart to those on the ride with us through life. When we listen with our hearts, we come to understand—wholly—what our partners in life are telling us. Armed with this enlightenment, we can secure ourselves above destructive struggle, even the paralysis of insecurity.

Often, this counsel runs us into a cul-de-sac because we misinterpret it as listening to the heart. Unfortunately, our hearts may reflect nothing more than momentary thoughts and desires; or they may be ruled by raging emotions or blinding fears or crippling events in our past. Our hearts may tell us that what feels right is right which isn't always right!

More helpful is to listen with the heart. Our hearts can guide us to what is central to our lives.

It's legendary that the indigenous people of the Americas used their exceptional sensitivity to nature to help them sense where danger lay in forest and plain, even where sustenance could be found. It was their critical "sixth sense," their means of survival. In some tribes, like the Muscogee Nation, they used this special sense to connect with others. Their greeting is extraordinarily instructive: "I am you being me." We share, in other words, the same spirit. We are one.

Many of us feel we have a sixth sense, the capacity to bond spiritually with others, to know where spiritual danger lurks and promise lies. We recall times when we have used our "powers" to get outside ourselves and inside others. That's listening with the heart. These powers of spiritual sensitivity appear to be built into the human frame; they can connect individuals intuitively with those with whom they live and work; and they can bring about spiritual wholeness. Simpler relationships, like those with young children, teach us how we can hear with our hearts and find spiritual union.

One day, I was waiting for my granddaughter, Sarah, to come out of preschool. As always, she ran to me and embraced me, but—this time—I could see that she was holding back tears. "What happened in school, sweetheart?" I asked. "Papa, Rachel said that I'm not her best friend anymore," she replied poignantly. Reflexively, I responded, "Well, you have other friends." NO! I had listened with my head, not with my heart. So I caught myself and continued, "You are hurt, aren't you, darling? Let me hold you." I sat down on the sidewalk and we hugged each other for several minutes. Then, we could speak about what to do next. We had connected — heart to heart.

Of course, adult relationships are often more complex, but the same principle applies: denying what others feel or brushing them aside is going in the wrong direction. Putting aside egos and scripted responses—listening with the heart—is taking the right step.

Connecting emotionally (empathizing), physically (drawing close and embracing), and spiritually (nurturing the Scend within and among us) are the three essentials to listening with the heart. They bring resolution. Telling Sarah not to be hurt discounted her feelings and disconnected us. Moving to eye-to-eye level, accepting her feelings, even adopting them as mine, opened the way to healing, and bonded us together. It's the ultimate validation that can be given to important others. "I share your hurt." "I feel your struggle." "I am you being me."

Listening with the heart triggers in lovers unbridled affection, in friends and colleagues remarkable care and profound respect, and with every companion, the deepest dimension of acceptance.

Listening with the heart enables couples in tension to withstand forces bent on pulling them apart. It leads to spiritual union. It ensures that we speak to each other from every possible perspective: heart and soul as well as mind and body. It makes two truly one.

Being joined from the heart with significant others also enables us to get off the path to self-fulfillment, a pathway that ultimately is divisive and unrewarding, and onto the broader road to joint fulfillment. It's difficult to get beyond self. But it can be accomplished once we make a habit of feeling what our partners in life feel, seeing the world through their eyes, reaching out through remarkable care and openness, once we make the sacred connection.

Those who listen with the heart typically hear "right" answers and do "right" things. Virtually all of us have the capacity for sacred connection, whatever our gender or role in life. And nearly all of us say we wish to live above relationship struggle, men as well as women. It's just as possible for a masculine man to be "softhearted" (open) as it is for a feminine woman to be hard-muscled. It turns out that being hard-muscled has value to some men and women; but being "softhearted" is the foundation for building rich and intuitive relationships—for everyone! Because of upbringing, culture, perhaps genetic makeup, this may be more difficult for some. Even so, it can be nurtured in virtually all sane folks. Those who are practiced in heart-to-heart communication insist it isn't hard to achieve. Virtually a glance, a gesture will do.

I learned this through an unforgettable encounter some years ago. I was staying with friends in the seacoast town of Soverato in southern Italy. As on past occasions, family, friends, neighbors—twenty or so—gathered around my host's dinner table on my first night there—laughing, enjoying each other's company, speaking of previous experiences together and what had transpired in the interim.

I noticed a different face, the face of a very shy young man. I was told that he was a distant relative from the north of Italy who had been so despondent, so overrun by the stress of losing a lover that he now didn't speak. He was invited to live with my friends in order to "find himself."

He was silent over nearly three hours of eating and celebrating. The next morning, as I was coming down the stairs, we made eye contact. Each day for a week, the same, but he didn't speak or even nod "hello." Nevertheless, I smiled at him and felt compelled to put my arms around him from time to time, saying, "Caro." (I care.)

One afternoon, to my surprise, he motioned to me to come outside and go in his car with him. He remained silent and mysterious as we drove into town. When he parked, he beckoned me to sit with him on a curb in front of a gelato shop. Suddenly, he spoke to me in an excited voice: "Hai mai avuto una granite Sicilia?" (Have you had Sicilian granita?) "No," I replied, "Che c'e'?" (What is it?) Into the shop he bounded and soon came out with a delicate mixture of lemon juice, sugar and lemon rind, all crystallized into a wonderfully refreshing ice. "Questa e meravigliosa" (This is marvelous!), I exclaimed.

We spoke together with extraordinary intensity about food and life for an hour or so and then returned home keeping our conversation going. My host, Paolo, was amazed. "What happened?" he asked. "Actually," I conjectured, "we've been talking to each other for a week—with our hearts."

Being open and sensitive doesn't necessitate spoken words. It does require an empathic reach from the heart. Sometime it's better to be silent. Words are not always revealing and, many times, people change their meaning into what they want to hear. We all know that face-to-face, heart-to-heart communication bonds people together; and it pulls them from struggle. It rises out of the spirit that makes us all human.

> Teach me to feel another's woe,
> To hide the fault I see;
> That mercy that I to others show,
> That mercy show to me.
>
> (Alexander Pope)

CHAPTER XV
STRATEGY FOUR:
HEAD INSIDE

PEOPLE SPEAK ABOUT HEARING from God in and through nature, or through miraculous, revelatory acts, or as a voice literally descending from heaven above. When we distill these accounts down to their essential experience, we come to recognize they are speaking of what they have heard, actually, from inside! After all, since Copernicus discovered that our earth goes around the sun, not the reverse, we know that God isn't literally above us listening for our pleas, our confessions, even our praise. God is, as our traditions teach us, omnipresent—within and among us— seeking union, bringing to those who respond new life, a new being, and new relationships—spiritual well-being.

How is this most vital connection made? Better, how is it hardwired, made constant? It's a particular challenge in today's helter-skelter world. Most of us lead many lives: we're workers – often of several jobs; we're parents and parents to parents; we're a taxi service; we're short-order cooks, tutors, solvers of all manner of problems, nurturers, financial advisors, social media addicts, and suppliers of any number of things. For this reason, we are not always clear about what anchors our lives, what provides focus, what grants meaning beyond the immediate, what we will look back on as significant in the last hours of our lives.

Unfortunately, not only are there a myriad of distractions in life, but some folks actually work to seal themselves off from their inner selves. Nearly four out of ten of those we surveyed indicated that they were "sometimes afraid to listen to the voice within."

I experienced this in dramatic fashion. I was trapped in a tiny ski hut near the top of Mt. Baldy in Southern California, alone with my thoughts for more than forty-eight hours, with no means of contacting others (no cell phones then!). An unexpected snowstorm had shut off my escape—first out the front door (the only door) and then to the single trail to civilization. I kept warm and filled with the only edibles left—tea and popcorn. Every *National Geographic* and *Reader's Digest* was read and reread; the cabin was cleaned as never before; and sleep stole much of the remainder of my time.

My thoughts were dominated by mundane, sometimes silly, reflections. Was my car, far below in the parking area, facing north or south? Was the lot paved or crushed rock? In time, solitude forced me to become my own companion, an unusual position for me! I found, to my surprise, that I wasn't ready to share much with my companion. I was about to make dramatic changes in my life, but I didn't use this rare opportunity to ponder these changes and their consequences. Upon reflection and with the objectivity the passage of time usually grants, I'm certain I was afraid to listen to my inner voice. I wasn't pleased with what it would say! Not long after, as time would prove, I made some very unwise decisions.

The voice inside can tell us who we are and what we're about; and it can tell us where we should go. Perhaps this is why, so often, we keep it at bay through life chatter and active daydreaming. To break in and connect, we have to become centered, disciplined, focused listeners. Then, the connection can be completed. In most traditions, the proven pathways inside are prayer, meditation, or, powerfully, what we might call centered reflection: letting distractions go, quieting emotions (especially those blocking communication), getting attuned to our essential selves, going to the Source—for people of faith, God's Spirit. When centered reflection becomes the first order of each day, it anchors life, clarifies who we are and who we can be. Those in our survey sample who describe themselves as spiritually strong agree with this statement: "When I am open, God speaks to me."

The ways of centered reflection (meditation, contemplation, prayer) are many. There is one paramount result—feeling union with our inner self. Centered reflection takes us past analyzing messages, past attempting to change them, and certainly past trying to escape them, to embracing them. For this reason, centered reflection heals; it transforms; it inspires; most important, it positively affects our outlook. Centered reflection transforms everyday living into inspired living, into the life the Apostle Paul speaks of in his letter to the Colossians, "putting on love which is the bond of perfectness" (3:14).

Spiritual well-being and centered reflection go hand-in-hand. A connected life keeps us on the right path because all paths are illuminated and seen for where they lead. It grants confidence, worth, direction. Disciplined, daily centered reflection brings a person's life picture into focus; and it enables each of us to find, within, the "Ultimate Friend."

Is this New Age theology, a departure from Christian traditions? On the contrary, it is at the heart of our traditions. This is not a call to extinguish the self or abandon faith; it is a call to discover one's authentic self and bond with the God who speaks to and through it. The spiritual life, in other words, does not come from obedience to external requirements of a foreign God outside the human frame, but from union with the God Within.

When people describe this journey of connection, they often speak of discovering, surprisingly and unexpectedly, a child within. Perhaps this is the meaning of Jesus' bold assertion that unless we become as little children, we cannot enter the kingdom of heaven (Matt. 18:3).

As it turns out we are never any particular age, birthdays and birth certificates aside. We always are children at heart. At sixteen years old, we are so often, ten in judgment and thirty in our desires. But as we progress through life, society melds these ages and interests together into one age—maturity. And this is good if we still have the child within. So for good reason we are, in our adult lives, rewarded at home, on the job, even by close friends for "acting adult": for being responsible, task-oriented, prudent, controlled and sober. Maturity means we know what is expected and what risky behaviors to avoid. Maturity is the theme of most therapy sessions.

Controlling speech and actions is sometimes like the experience I've had reading from a teleprompter on television. Yes, my statements are concise and exact, but they also can be heard as forced and unnatural, at times even insincere, especially if someone else has scripted them for me. Better in life to add the child back in — to speak and act naturally, freely, playfully.

It can be argued the family that plays together stays together. When people routinely and not so routinely engage in simple playfulness, when they expose the child within and bring that child into their relationships, they reconnect with their inner selves and overcome inauthenticity, even the threats of injustice, insecurity, and insincerity. Discovering and engaging the child within is extraordinarily healing. It's a potent therapy. It relieves stress; it unveils options not always possible in structured adult reality; and it expands our understanding of self. As Jesus counseled his disciples, "whoever receives a child in my name, receives me" (Luke 9:48).

There are many ways to release the playful nature. One

sure way is simply to act like a child. Get down on the floor, roll around, sing fun songs, have inspirations, "smell the roses"— preferably with little children. Act silly, tease dogs and adults, speak nonsense—even in loud tones. Hug in public, frolic in the snow, roll in piles of leaves, wear grubby clothes, let out pent-up feelings, and let in the fun of life.

Acting like a child brings spontaneity back into life and lets out the guileless, constructive self within. For these reasons and perhaps as a carryover from my Italian heritage, I have a special love of "extreme" challenges—skiing expert slopes (not as an expert), kayaking through giant ice floes on the perilous Grand River of Ohio in early springtime, surfing Hawaii's mammoth waves on a red flag day. Perhaps it comes from years of daily adventure with my son and now with my grandchildren nearly every day. But it also stems from paying heed to a mountain of research that shows that, while modern society has thrust its citizens progressively into a tightly molded regimen (the conformity of adulthood), fulfillment and contentment come from breaking the mold, living and relating spontaneously and joyfully, splicing childlike fun into every endeavor.

Peggy and Margaret, two college professors (can you think of any role more serious and straitlaced?) taught me early in my professional life how the child within us can bring relief to the serious side of life, and energize others. Two very different women — one conservative, early forties, a perfect model of Talbot's finest; the other a staunch liberal, fifties, matronly in appearance — team-taught U.S. history to crowded auditoriums of eager and enthusiastic students.

Why their extraordinary appeal? (Students rarely clamor to take history.) It was their playfulness! They fanned the winds of gossip, featured the foibles and eccentricities of our nation's leaders, one and all. They satirized each other's dearly held positions, engaged students in mock battles, ridiculed heroes, and strutted the classroom with provocation and abandon. They celebrated the child within them and drew out the child within their students: demystifying the obscure, liberating curiosity, turning ardor into play. And best of all, they held their students to the last seat in the back row and to the last day—captive! They taught me that even the most serious considerations can bring us joy when "adult" allows in "child."

Of course, we're not speaking of impulsive, out-of-control, anti-social behavior, but of open, good-natured spontaneity that builds and enhances caring relationships. It is paradoxical but, in uncanny ways, people can smile even in the face of great tragedy if they act out as a child.

It's never too late to have a happy childhood. It's never too late to make the inner connection. It's the threshold of spiritual well-being.

So, looking back over the commitments, spiritual well-being moves from the inside out and is expressed in caring, open relationships—in a word, in love.

Seventy-two percent of our survey respondents agree. When they are moved from the inside, they are able to find peace and feel whole—spiritually and emotionally. The majority of those studied say this is the way God reveals himself to them" and grants to them a new life. As important, they believe they deserve the new life that comes from making the inside connection,' a life above destructive struggle. There is—and should be—no guilt here!

CHAPTER XVI
LIVING ABOVE THE STRUGGLES"

A STRANGE AND REVEALING STORY IS sandwiched into the book of Genesis, just after Noah and the flood and immediately before a recounting of Abraham's ancestry: the Tower of Babel story (Gen. 11:1-9). Strange, because we find God alarmed that nomads wandering the desert plan to settle down and build a tower that would reach into heaven. Revealing, because the storyteller clearly believes these desert wanderers could do such a thing. In fact, according to the account, so likely were they to succeed that God decided to scramble their speech in order to interrupt their work. Apparently, the author and early hearers of the story thought that God resides directly above, perhaps on a canopy just a few hundred feet above their settlements.

The story, of course ancient, provides a clue to how people over millennia have visualized the spiritual landscape: God, separate from humanity, is above though not too far away to ensure he can listen in and at times intervene. Close enough, as well, to maintain command.

Here's the message: To find spiritual well-being, humans must send praise and pleas "heavenward" while being careful to be earthbound—obedient, humble, docile, tethered down here. The ambition, the striving that drove these settlers to challenge heaven, must be supplanted by acquiescence to the constraining will of God. Then, and only then, will a positive connection with God be secured.

Over the centuries since the Babel story's recounting, people have been sent on a myriad of spiritual migrations—from guru to guru, experience to experience—in search of the power line to heaven, God's plan for the world, God's plan for their lives. These journeys usually have led to disappointment and heightened spiritual struggle. The faithful connect in special moments with the God beyond but—no matter how committed⁻soon disconnect because they are earthbound. They do God's will—then fall short of God's expectations. Like the wildebeests of Africa's Serengeti Plain, these seekers are on spiritual migrations looking for sustenance and security, but they are never out of reach of predators. They hope for strength, but they become exhausted by the journey itself. They are certain security and justice come through judgment from above, that the God on high will reassure and secure them, that they will find authentic living through a divinely imposed life agenda. With only a fragile link to the Almighty beyond, however, they fall short time and again — and so they struggle.

When we asked people to describe spiritual well-being, invariably they spoke of life "above destructive struggles," "a gold standard in living," "finding in every waking moment the power that affirms and grants purpose and meaning." They spoke of living through inspiration —Scend. And when we asked the saints among us how that power is experienced in everyday life, they often talked in poetic terms: of smelling the sweet fragrance (Scent) of spiritual living, of inner delight balancing out their otherwise mundane lives. They related stories of exhilaration, hope, optimism, care, and strength.

I interviewed lyanla Vanzant early in her publishing career. A few minutes into our discussion, I knew she wasn't another woman with a book. Iyanla was on her way by New York transit to pick up her welfare check when she read on an advertising panel over her seat: "Create a Better Future. Come to Medgar Evers College." She did. "I'm out of here," she exclaimed, "out of welfare, on to college." How could she fashion such a turnaround? She felt, she shared with me, compelled to take a journey of faith. "It's in our blood, in our genes; we have designer genes," she exclaimed. Her language was impassioned, intuitive, provocative; her message — a-Scending.

Those who feel spiritually energized, like Iyanla, report consistently that they look inside to break the bonds of spiritual struggle. We conclude, therefore: transformation occurs when connected people release the power within them.

One of the great enigmas of Christian history is how believers go about releasing the "Spirit of Christ" into their lives. Prayer has been one obligatory methodology—personal and congregational. The assumption is that the God above releases his Spirit to those below—on request. So whatever the tradition, whether as pleas or recitations, prayers are offered with the hope the Receiver—external to the world—can and will listen in and become the Responder. The language of prayer often makes this clear. God is addressed as "above," "beyond," "on high," and, descriptively, with the power to intervene—"the Almighty" "Ruler of the Universe,' Creator," "Savior." Even when using intimate, familial language — e.g., "Father" and "Dear" — those offering prayers plead for the presence of the God transcendent.

Inspiration, however, isn't "called in" from the outside. Inspiration, in a word, is not mediated by prayer, even through the church. It is immediate.

That's its most essential quality.

CHAPTER XVII
STRATEGY FIVE:
LIVING INSPIRED

THE VOICES OF OUR TRADITIONS TELL us powerfully that spiritual well-being is expressed in our demeanor, most significantly, in transforming connections that come by way of inspiration. In fact, people from many cultures and almost all of the world's great religions (except Buddhism) speak of the dignity of the soul and the nobility and resilience of the human spirit, and of hearing the inner voice of God's spirit. Perhaps this speech is mythological, but— especially in Western traditions—these words are understood by most followers to describe the core of our emotions, the seat of individual enlightenment, and the source of our personal strength. They speak of a power that people of all levels of sophistication— particularly, the saints among us—say they have claimed, at least witnessed, in this book called Scend:

A surge from within that heals, resolves and inspires us.

When everyday folks put detail to this experience, they talk about being open to the still, small, but awe-inspiring voice of God inside; of embracing others— even strangers—through empathy and compassion; of connecting with their essential selves, the sacred, and with God. They speak of healing breaches in relationships, of becoming one with others, of acting redemptively, not judgmentally. And they speak of being empowered to live above struggle.

It's reasonable to conclude that spiritual power, life-changing energy, is present, perhaps in the human community, certainly in those who are inspired. The shared human spirit is the spirit that has enabled many oppressed to endure great suffering; it's the spirit that has allowed many who have been victimized to demonstrate uncommon valor, to create remarkable beauty, even to advance the human condition. We have a high calling. It is to share the bounty of the human spirit.

Although women in our survey recognized the significance of Scend two to one over their male counterparts, most everyone identified with a "Yes" within, with a power rising spontaneously from joining aspiration with inspiration, with being vaulted forward as by a great wave.

Embracing the God Within brings a new perspective on life and the spiritual well-being we seek. And what are the results? When people embrace the God Within, they do what is intrinsically good — and they don't take away the opportunity of others to be good in the same way. That is extremely important! They become the "salt of the earth." Their faith becomes activated in everyday living. As John Wesley is reported to have whispered as his final words, "The best of all is this that God is with us."

The world of peace and unity that modern peoples have clamored for and achieved by tearing off the chains of those who have been enslaved, tearing down the walls that have separated and imprisoned many, through political action, commerce, and military might can also come about by simply accepting the vision of the Sermon on the Mount, the hope that love and Scend will cover us all and enable us to be, above all, peacemakers.

The story of Dorothy in the Land of Oz comes to mind. She struggled to get back to her kinfolk in Kansas, traveling under great duress from Munchkinland to the Emerald City only to discover on the last page of her journey that her return to Kansas was within her power from her very first steps on the yellow brick road. Dorothy in The Wizard of Oz learned—finally—from Glenda, the Good Witch: "You've always had the power to go home! As colorful, exciting, and anguishing as her dreamline to the Emerald City had been, as perplexing as her encounter with the Wizard was, she already was back in Kansas—all she needed to do to escape her nightmare was Wake Up!

The saints among us describe their discovery of spiritual well-being in the same terms: finding what is resident within, transcending struggle through healing transforming relationships, awakening to experience that lighthearted lilt we feel when we have gone to the beach on an early summer day. It is Scend!

Struggles of spirituality transform into manageable challenges when Scend-filled relationships become primary, when we act from compassion and conscience, build from strengths and positive events. When we act from our inmost selves, our deeply embedded hopes and dreams come alive. We are inner-directed and propelled; and we joyfully exult in our newfound state of spiritual well-being.

Liberation from fears of the world

Openness to our inmost selves

Expansion of our circle of comfort

The hope, the lilt of springtime

The color, the crisp of autumn

God with us in all seasons.

CHAPTER XVIII
SUSTAINING THE
TRANSCENDENT LIFE

A N ACRID SMELL, THEN SCREAMS, FILLED the air. I was in the office of the president of the Borough of Manhattan Community College on a bright November day, looking out from seven stories up at a million tons of ugly rubble and a thousand firefighters protesting their removal from their fallen buddies. They no longer were needed, Mayor Giuliani directed. A confrontation between comrades—police and fire— was unfolding. It was 2001! Already traumatized office workers were certain a bloody riot was imminent. They couldn't hold back their fright, their anguish. They had witnessed enough mayhem. They had to <u>call</u> out in pain.

I met beautiful but fragile people that day. They had seen the horrific explosions, felt the earth shake, and then shake again; they had witnessed friends and strangers running in panic, falling to their deaths from the World Trade Center towers. They had endured nearly two months of continuous, life-crushing disruptions—loss of phones and power and e-mail, and of lives. Their days were endless, their nights sleepless. Demands never placed before on leaders of any American college came at them in relentless waves. They were emotionally spent, physically fatigued, spiritually drained.

I had come to hear their stories, to understand their plight, and to fathom their strength and resilience. The blows of the terrorists they still were enduring, but their spirits were undamaged: a painter who stayed on the job all night September 11 to help set up and run a triage center; the chief of public safety whose staff remained for days, though under siege, to keep the campus intact; a wonderful nurse who treated scores wounded mainly in soul; the public relations director who rose and continued to rise to a barrage of administrator, faculty and student calls for explanation and assistance; the media director assigned to me with his student crew, shaken, weary, but so professional, so eager to serve; and a professor with healing in her heart, Dr. Susan Horowitz.

Fancy degrees from Chicago, Yale, and New York University aside, this professor of English warmed my heart, spoke to me—heart to heart—of courage, of resilience, of the nobility of the human spirit, and of trust, belief, empathy, centered reflection— overwhelmingly, of inspiration. She had a-Scended above the terrible struggles of the moment, struggles that had torn away her defenses and brought a pent-up world of hurts to the surface. "Don't mind my hair," she explained. "I'm not going to get it cut until my hairdresser starts back her salon. It's the least I can do for her."

I've met a number of saints, certainly my mentor and teacher, Dr. Don Clifton, but also this petite but immensely strong educator, Susan. Her stylist was still shut down, but her manicurist had come back to work. An immigrant from China working long hours— mostly in silence (she could speak little English)—she responded when Susan reached out "by impulse" to her. "Would you like a better life?" Susan gestured. "I don't have time for classes," she conveyed in word and through awkward hand movements. "Well, I'm going to teach you myself," Susan offered. "Do you like music? Then sing with me." Lesson One was under way: "You are my sunshine, my only sunshine. You make me happy when skies are gray..." As she related this story, we together broke out into singing: "You'll never know, dear, how much I love you. Please don't take that sunshine away."

There were four Asian immigrant manicurists in the shop. Soon, every week, they sang together. Every week they learned more English. Every week they built trust. They felt Susan's remarkable empathy and compassion; they were inspired; they experienced the uplifting power of Scend.

The Scend-power I felt years ago when my mentor, the dean, reached out in Christian compassion to warm a lost and homeless soul, I witnessed this November day at Ground Zero.

Of course, we don't have to survive a terrorist attack to be spiritually energized. It requires—simply— connections, strong connections

    *with one's primal self;
    *with those who come into view, even for a

few moments—the humble as well as the powerful;

*with what is sacred; and

*with the God who elevates our lives.

As the Jewish philosopher Martin Buber wrote a generation ago, "All real living is meeting."'

To have spiritual well-being is to be transformed from primal insecurity, destructive inauthenticity, from being alone—to being cradled by the Spirit that binds us together and grants meaning, indeed high purpose, to our lives. Achieving spiritual well-being is moving from debilitating struggle to confident victory, from the rubble of life into the field of flowers of inspired living.

Susan occupies for me a pontifical seat of spiritual well-being. She and thousands of other inspired rescuers and preservers have taught us what is of lasting value and inherent virtue: human resilience spiced with large doses of kindness, powered by Scend, the unquenchable fire within. Susan teaches us that we must make—in thought and action—a paradigm shift: from searching for salvation from the God beyond to living redemptively through the God Within.

Susan and millions of others have discovered that when we live out commitment to a higher cause we gain that healing sense of well-being. I've been a community college president for many years. If there is anything I've learned through years of experiences it's that the single greatest reward I've gained is inspiring and leading others to living above their struggles: gaining great self-confidence, a productive career and life, the American dream. It's what led me to this powerful movement in higher education and driven my efforts throughout my career.

Of course, life—even powered by Scend—isn't a continuous whoosh. We don't always act as we should and for others. We disappoint. Struggles are an inescapable part of life. Waves can wondrously glide us beachward, but, sometimes, when we jump the next, we go up against a maelstrom of forces and we're thrown off course. The good news is that, in the end, each effort can build resilience and ultimately affirmation.

I'm always struck by the extraordinary excitement that first-of-their-family college students exhibit when they come to know that they, too, can succeed—even in competition with the children of our best educated and most successful citizens. The same excitement and empowerment are present with those who come to experience the power of spiritual living and celebrate this new reality. Overcoming life's many struggles in the twenty-first century comes down to spiritual surfing — taking life's powerful waves to the serenity of foam and sand.

Now as they often say to newlyweds in Italy:

> *Avanti con effusione*—Go forward with Spirit!

APPENDIX A
THE RESEARCH BASE

THE RESPONSES TO SURVEYS of 486 adult Americans selected to mirror anticipated readers (those in search of spiritual well-being) undergird this book. Some in the sample say they are already models of spiritual strength. Their responses were separated out and scrutinized to determine common traits and commitments. The instrument used is the Index of Spirituality developed by the author in consultation with Dr. Donald Clifton, longtime chair and CEO of The Gallup Organization (see Appendix B). Index questions were derived from comments of more than twelve hundred participants in seventy-six focus groups who related real-life stories about spiritual struggles and victories over them. Focus group participants identified what was holding them back (their struggles), then they ranked these struggles in order of life importance. Finally, they talked through strategies they have found effective in overcoming spiritual struggle or have witnessed in others. Those individuals who spoke of and exhibited what we call Scend in their lives were sorted out from the others so the ingredients of the Scend experience could be identified and clarified. The Five Commitments described in the book, however, derive from survey analysis. These commitments correlate with perceived individual spirituality.

APPENDIX B
THE LITERATURE

OUR PATHWAY TO SPIRITUAL well-being includes perspectives from philosophy, psychology, and both Western and Eastern traditions. This does not represent an abandonment of the Christian faith. Christian thought accepted, early on, the conceptual framework of Greek philosophy and was enhanced, not undermined, by it. We can grow—and we should—from all spiritually constructive approaches.

The extensive professional literature on happiness, flow, and life satisfaction was carefully studied —from Clifton to Seligman to Kahneman to Diener to Emmons to Csikszentmihalyi. These often labeled "positive psychologists" were helpful. They have linked spirituality to subjective well-being; but they have not set forth how the formidable challenges to spiritual well-being (the struggles) can be overcome.

APPENDIX C
FOCUS GROUP RESEARCH

IT TOOK A NUMBER OF FOCUS GROUPS centered on life struggles—of college students, church members, and conference attendees—to realize that spiritual well-being was a key to the understanding of all life struggles, whatever one's age, gender, race, socioeconomic level, or religious preference.

Once it was recognized that the ultimate struggles were with connections—with oneself, important others, what we believe to be sacred, and then subsequent focus groups zeroed in on issues of life purpose, security, authenticity, and transforming connections: spirituality.

www.ingramcontent.com/pod-product-compliance
Lightning Source LLC
Chambersburg PA
CBHW072127090426
42739CB00012B/3090